simply BEAUTIFUL BOXES

DOUG STOWE

POPULAR WOODWORKING BOOKS
CINCINNATI, OHIO
www.popularwoodworking.com

READ THIS IMPORTANT SAFETY NOTICE

To prevent accidents, keep safety in mind while you work. Use the safety guards installed on power equipment; they are for your protection. When working on power equipment, keep fingers away from saw blades, wear safety goggles to prevent injuries from flying wood chips and sawdust, wear headphones to protect your hearing, and consider installing a dust vacuum to reduce the amount of airborne sawdust in your woodshop. Don't wear loose clothing, such as neckties or shirts with loose sleeves, or jewelry, such as rings, necklaces or bracelets, when working on power equipment. Tie back long hair to prevent it from getting caught in your equipment. People who are sensitive to certain chemicals should check the chemical content of any product before using it. The author and editors who compiled this book have tried to make the contents as accurate and correct as possible. Plans, illustrations, photographs and text have been carefully checked. All instructions, plans and projects should be carefully read, studied and understood before beginning construction. Due to the variability of local conditions, construction materials, skill levels, etc., neither the author nor Popular Woodworking Books assumes any responsibility for any accidents, injuries, damages or other losses incurred resulting from the material presented in this book.

METRIC CONVERSION CHART

TO CONVERT	TO	MULTIPLY BY
Inches	Centimeters	2.54
Centimeters	Inches	0.4
Feet	Centimeters	30.5
Centimeters	Feet	0.03
Yards	Meters	0.9
Meters	Yards	1.1
Sq. Inches	Sq. Centimeters	6.45
Sq. Centimeters	Sq. Inches	0.16
Sq. Feet	Sq. Meters	0.09
Sq. Meters	Sq. Feet	10.8
Sq. Yards	Sq. Meters	0.8
Sq. Meters	Sq. Yards	1.2
Pounds	Kilograms	0.45
Kilograms	Pounds	2.2
Ounces	Grams	28.4
Grams	Ounces	0.04

 Published by Popular Woodworking Books, an imprint of F&W Publications, Inc., 1507 Dana Avenue, Cincinnati, Ohio, 45207. First edition.

Visit our Web site at www.popularwoodworking.com for information on more resources for woodworkers.

Other fine Popular Woodworking Books are available from your local bookstore or direct from the publisher.

05 04 03 02 01 6 5 4 3 2

Library of Congress Cataloging-in-Publication Data

Stowe, Doug.
Simply beautiful boxes / by Doug Stowe -- 1st ed.
p. cm.
Includes index.
ISBN 1-55870-514-7 (alk. paper)
1. Woodwork. 2. Wooden boxes. I. Title: Beautiful boxes. II. Title.
TT200.S73 2000 99-055028
745.593--dc21 CIP

Edited by Michael Berger
Cover designed by Brian Roeth
Cover photography by Al Parrish
Interior photography by Doug Stowe
Production coordinated by Sara Dumford
Computer illustrations by Doug Stowe and Melanie Powell

About the Author

Doug Stowe is a professional furniture designer/craftsman and box maker who lives with his wife, Jean, and daughter, Lucy, on a wooded hillside overlooking Eureka Springs, Arkansas. He is the author of *Creating Beautiful Boxes With Inlay Techniques*. His furniture has been featured in *Woodworker's Journal* and *Fine Woodworking,* and his work can be found online at www.dougstowe.com.

PHOTO BY RICHARD OWEN

Acknowledgments

My thanks to:

My wife, Jean, inspiring, and enthusiastic!

My daughter, Lucy, creative and fun!

Mike Berger and the staff at Popular Woodworking Books.

John Behrle, Woodcraft Supply.

Cliff Paddock, Jesada Tools.

Pete Spooler, Klingspor's Sanding Catalogue.

The friends and customers that have kept me busy and sustained doing work that I love.

Jewelry shown in photographs courtesy of Magee Jewelry, Eureka Springs, Arkansas

Dedication

To those who cherish and protect our hardwood forests.

Table of Contents

Introduction

Woodworking is a process of story telling. A single piece of wood can tell what type of tree it came from and where, what the soil and climate were like where it grew—in short, the story of its life. A woodworker takes the wood and adds his or her own story, expressing a level of understanding of material and tools, recording in the wood as if in a journal, the evolution of personal values and the narrative of his or her growth as a craftsman.

Woodworking is a way of telling who and what we are as human beings in a language that speaks more clearly and with greater patience and sincerity than words alone.

Jewelry boxes are personal. Often when I'm set up at a show to sell my work, people will look at the jewelry boxes I've made and say, "Your wife must have a beautiful jewelry box." "Well, no," I respond, "she's waiting for just the right one." The awful truth is that my wife, Jean, stores her jewelry in a plastic organizer she bought at Wal-Mart. I had given her a jewelry chest years ago, but when a gallery called asking about it, Jean said, "Sell mine." We needed the money, so the fiddleback maple jewelry chest with walnut pulls was sold and has yet to be replaced. I keep trying.

Jewelry boxes are expressions of relationship. A story told of love, of commitment, of sharing, of understanding, of listening, of knowing. We are each unique in our needs and in what we express. While one woman (or man) may wear earrings, another rings, another necklaces, another pins, or some mix of all, it is a challenge to design jewelry boxes that meet the unique needs of an individual without getting personal.

It is also a challenge to offer designs suited to the unique abilities of various craftsmen. Jewelry boxes can be very simple or as complicated as any large piece of furniture.

Some can be done with a limited selection of tools, while others require elaborate operations with complicated setups and a high degree of precision. You may want to make something you find here. Feel free to make changes and personalize these designs.

Choose woods that have meaning for you and let your selection of materials become part of your adventure in woodworking. You may wish to use this book to begin discussions with a loved one to guide you in making a box of your own design that tells a more personal story of a loving relationship. If you are a beginner, you may want to start with some of the simpler projects and work your way toward more complicated boxes as your skills develop.

My own woodworking is a story about relationship with wood, a love for grain and color (mainly brown) and texture and scent. (Have you ever smelled sassafras?) A love also for the forest and wild things that live there and toward which I feel a reverence and a desire to protect. One of these days my work with wood will lead me to create the perfect jewelry box for Jean. I hope my efforts on these pages will be useful to you and that the story my woodworking tells may help you to better understand yourself.

Many of the more complicated projects in this book require more steps than can reasonably be recorded in the limited amount of space available. Fortunately, for most of the projects, and as you gain personal experience in woodworking, "next" steps will make themselves known to you as your project evolves.

I remind my readers that copyright laws are written to protect artists from being copied in the marketplace, and that my sharing the designs and techniques used in my work does not grant license to produce these pieces for sale. Your own personal growth will be best served by allowing what I offer here to stimulate and inspire work of your own design.

There is a saying that the teacher's work is completed when his students surpass him. Some of you will accept the challenge and opportunity that wood offers of reaching toward excellence, personal expression and growth. It is you for whom I write in the knowledge that you will surpass me.

Chapter 1

Inlaid Walnut Ring Box

Woodworking techniques evolve over time. My first boxes were made with simple butt joints and glue. Many have withstood years of use, showing that woodworking can be done to a level of enjoyment and satisfaction with projects less complicated than this box. Like most craftsmen, however, I can't help making things better where I can. The simple mortise-and-tenon technique makes this box strong enough to withstand generations of use, and its bottom panel is free-floating to expand and contract with seasonal changes.

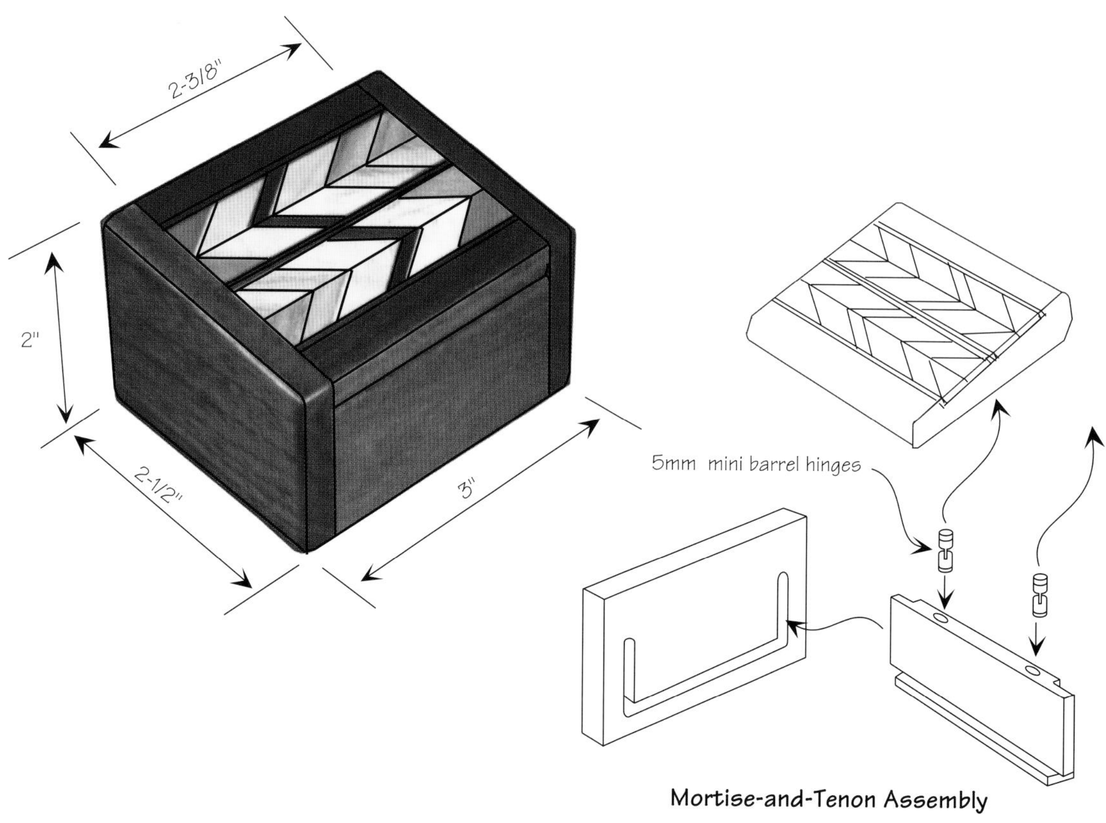

Mortise-and-Tenon Assembly

Bill of Materials

PART NAME	NUMBER	DIMENSION TWL	COMMENTS
Ends	2	5/16" x 2" x 2 9/16"	
Front	1	5/16" x 1 5/16" x 2 5/8"	
Back	1	5/16" x 1 5/16" x 2 5/8"	
Bottom	1	5/16" x 2 1/16" x 2 19/32"	
Top	1	7/8" x 2 9/16" x 3"	Resawn at angle from stock. Cut to fit dimension of finished box.
Hardware			
Mini Barrel Hinges	1 pair	5mm	

Make the Inlay

Inlay is a good starting point for play and experimentation. This herringbone inlay is simple for a beginner and is often used as inlay banding on furniture. On this box, I decided that two strips would best fill the space available on top.

Glue strips of wood into a larger block. The final pattern will be more interesting if the strips are of varying widths. I frequently utilize offcut strips from other projects. The strips need to have two dimensions roughly in common: thickness and length. Joint the edges of the strips to get good gluing surfaces. Spread glue layer by layer; then, using hardwood strips to distribute the pressure, clamp the strips tightly together. I use a thick hardwood strip on one side to make sure the block will come out straight.

On the jointer, level one side of the block, and square one edge. On the table saw, cut the opposite side of the block so that it is uniform in width. Use the cutoff sled to cut the block into angled pieces (photo 1). The cut-off sled allows the use of clamps to hold very small parts. Then, using the table saw and rip fence, cut side banding strips about 3⁄32" thick. I used walnut to make the strip blend with the box top.

Arrange the angled pieces on the banding strips, and glue them in place. I apply a layer of glue to the angled piece and banding strip as they are laid in place (photo 2). Use the bar clamps and hardwood strips from earlier to clamp the inlay together (photo 3).

After the glue has dried, use the jointer to clean up one edge of the new inlay block. Use a thin-kerf carbide blade in the table saw to cut strips of finished inlay from the block (photo 4). The strips should be ripped to about 3⁄32" thick, allowing for the inlay to have a thickness of at least 1⁄16" after final sanding.

Prepare the Box Stock

Cut the rough walnut stock to about ¼" over finished width. Rip the front and back separately from the ends and bottom. Use the band saw and fence to

1 **To make the inlay, start with a block of wood laminated from layers of various hardwoods. Use a cutoff sled on the table saw with temporary fences nailed or screwed in place.**

2 **Align the angled pieces that were cut from the laminated block into place along the walnut backing strips. Apply glue to both sides as the parts are laid in position.**

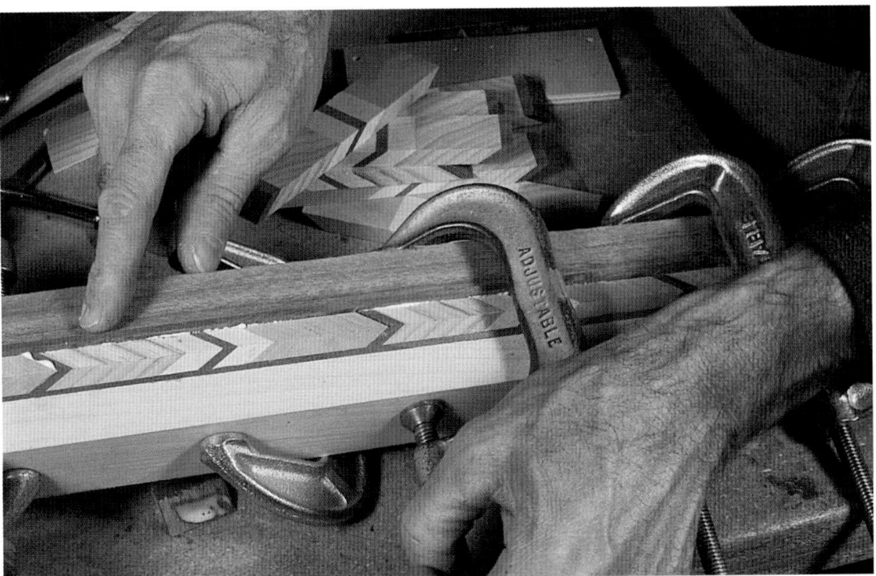

3 **Use hardwood backing strips and C-clamps to glue the inlay block together. The backing blocks will keep the assembly straight, saving work later.**

4 Before beginning to rip the 3/32" inlay strips, I used the jointer to flatten one side of the block. A push stick keeps the fingers safe from the saw blade.

5 On the router table, use a 1/8" straight-cut bit to rout the mortises for the front and back of the box. The three pieces in the photo show the three-step progression, left to right, for routing the mortises.

6 To rout the tenons for the box front and back, use a 1" straight-cut bit in the router table. Here I have the safety blocking removed to show the cutter. Photo 7 shows the safety blocking in place.

7 Check the fit of the mortise and tenon. A perfect fit will hold against gravity even without glue. Note the safety blocking securely clamped to the router table.

resaw the 1"-thick (4/4) walnut stock. I use a wide blade on the band saw, adjusting the angle of the fence to allow for the natural inclination of the blade.

Plane the walnut stock to 5/16" thick, then joint one edge. Rip the stock to approximately 1/32" over finished width, and then joint the other side to bring it to the final dimension.

Cut the parts to length on the table saw, using the 90° angle sled or sliding table. Clamp a stop block to the fence so the parts will be exactly equal in length. Cut the ends to length first, then change the location of the stop block to cut the front and back. For the bottom panel, loosen the clamp holding the stop block in place and bump the stop block over about 1/32". This way the bottom will have just a tiny bit of end-to-end clearance when assembled.

Cut the Mortises and Tenons

Cut the mortises and tenons on the router table. Because the router bit used for cutting the mortises is a fixed width, cut the mortises first, then cut the tenons to fit.

Install the 1/8" straight-cut router bit. Set the fence 11/32" from the outside tip of the router bit. This measurement is the approximate width of the walnut stock plus 1/32" cleanup allowance, which will be sanded away when the box is completed. Adjust the height of cut to just barely over 1/8". Cut a test piece, and check the dimensions and depth with a dial caliper. Once you are satisfied the measurements are correct, clamp stop blocks to the fence to control the width of the mortise. Rout the ends so that the front, back and bottom panels fit. This requires changing the locations of the stop blocks and routing in three separate operations. Fortunately, the depth of cut and fence position remain the same, and only the stop positions require adjustment (photo 5).

To rout the tenons to size, use a 1" straight-cut bit, climb-feeding the piece

8 Using the same setup, shape the bottom panel to fit.

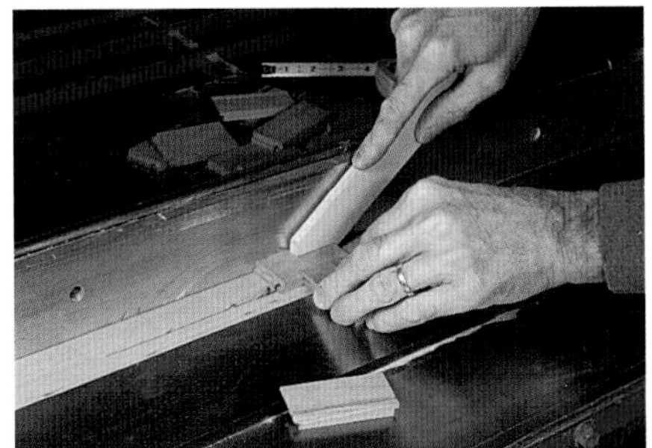

9 While cutting the dadoes, a push stick keeps my fingers away from the blade. I also use a block of wood to keep the workpiece against the fence.

10 Use the sled on the table saw to cut the tenons to width. This involves cutting off the little nub below the dado that the bottom will fit into. Use a stop block to accurately position the cut.

11 To cut the channel for the inlay, use a 1" straight-cut bit in the router table. Gradually widen the cut until you reach the desired width. Cut the channel first, then size the inlay to fit.

from right to left along the fence (photo 6). In climb-feeding, the workpiece is moved from right to left between the fence and the cutter. This gives a cleaner cut with little tear-out, but can be dangerous with a dull cutter. Safety blocking is required to keep fingers from being pulled into the cutter. Always rout a test piece to make certain you've set the height of the cutter at ⅛". The fit to the mortise is best tested by actual fit rather than measuring. Insert the tenon into the mortise. If it goes in easily without forcing but doesn't fall out without shaking it, the fit is perfect and, with a spot of glue will last many years (photo 7).

Using the same setup as used for the tenons, rout the edges of the bottom panel. Check the fit of the panel to the dadoes cut into the end pieces, and adjust the fence if necessary (photo 8).

Use a ⅛"-kerf blade on your table saw to cut the dadoes in the front and back pieces for the bottom panel to fit into. Set the fence so that the cut will be ⅛" deep and leave a 1" interior space. The front and back will be flush with the bottom when assembled (photo 9).

In order for the tenons to fit the mortises, small nubs must be cut off. I use the sled on the table saw with the blade lowered so that it just cuts through the thickness of the nub. The stop block is set so that the saw cut is flush with the routed tenon shoulder (photo 10).

Make the Lid

Plane walnut stock to ⅞" thick and ¹⁄₁₆" wider than the planned width of the box. Tilt the band saw table, and adjust the fence to resaw the angled lid. With the help of a straightedge, draw the desired lid shape on the end of the stock. Then compare the pencil mark to where the blade will hit the stock when held up to the band saw.

Make a trial cut, barely penetrating one end of the stock. Turn the stock

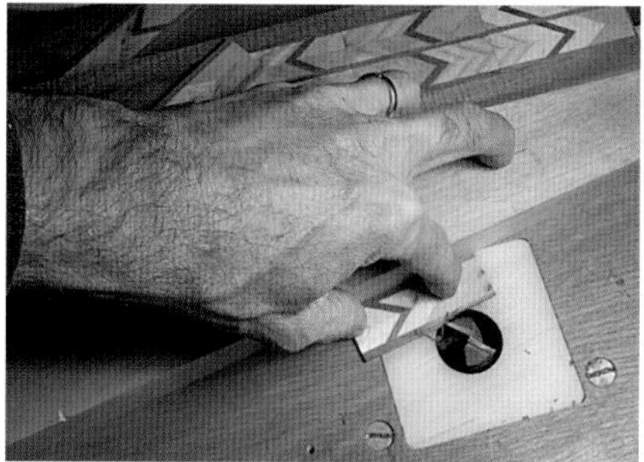

12 Adjust the distance between the router bit and fence on the router table, then trim the inlay to fit the channel. Use safety blocking, which was removed for this photo to illustrate the procedure.

13 Spread glue in the routed channel and press the inlay strips in place.

14 In my production work, I clamp two lids face-to-face with a filler strip between them to distribute clamping pressure and to keep the lids from sticking to each other.

over to see if the cut aligns. If not, you may have to adjust the fence. When you are satisfied that the cut is at the center of the stock, cut the lid stock into two parts. One part will become the lid, but you will need the other part when you drill for the hinges later in this chapter.

Inlay the Lid

Cut the channel for the inlay to fit into. Use the 1" straight-cut bit in the router table. Raise the height of the cut to just under the thickness of the inlay. Adjust the fence so that the first cut occurs at the center of the lid. Widen the channel with a second cut. For the final cut, make the channel about ¼" narrower than the combined width of two inlay strips. This last cut is achieved by passing the lid material from left to right on the router table. The reason for this is to keep the router bit from grabbing the stock and dangerously pulling it into the cutter (photo 11).

Cut the inlay strips about ¼" longer than the planned length of the lids, and pass them across the jointer to straighten one edge. Use the jointer to remove enough stock so that the final fitting will leave the border equal on both sides.

Raise the height of the bit in the router table until it is just taller than the thickness of the inlay. Move the fence so that it will cut the inlay strip to size. Safety blocking is a very good idea, helping to keep fingers well away from contact with the router bit. Clamp the safety blocking onto the router table with C-clamps. I prefer to make the first cut a bit wide, narrowing the width between the cutter and fence on a trial-and-error basis until I get it right (photo 12). Spread glue in the routed channel and place the inlay (photo 13). Clamp the inlay to the lid using a filler strip to distribute the clamping pressure (photo 14).

Fit and Hinge the Lid

For this box, I chose the readily available 5mm miniature barrel hinges which require a 45° chamfer to provide clearance for opening.

Use the sled on the table saw to cut the box top to length. Gauge the dimensions of the box opening with a tape measure, and set the stop block accordingly. Make the first cut on the right side of the lid, and the second after moving the lid against the stop block. Trial-assemble the box to test the fit. Bump the stop block over in small increments to make any adjustments (photo 15).

With a 5mm brad-point bit in the drill press, adjust the fence so that the bit will drill right into the center thickness of the 5⁄16" back piece. Use the dial caliper to check the open length of the mini barrel hinges. The depth of the holes should be slightly less than half the open length of the barrel hinge. Adjust the stop to the right depth, and drill a test piece. Check the depth of the hole with the pin end of the dial caliper (photo 16). To position the back piece for drilling, clamp a stop block to the fence. Using a piece of scrap wood, also drill an index piece that will be used to locate the proper position for

15 Trial-assemble your box, then cut the lid to size. A stop block clamped to the sled fence, adjusting to get the perfect fit, gives accurate results.

16 Stop blocks clamped on the fence of your drill press allow accurate drilling for 5mm mini barrel hinges. Drill precisely in the center thickness of the back piece.

17 To set up for drilling the matching holes in the lid, drill an index piece. Check the dimensions with a dial caliper. To help position the stop blocks, the index piece should start the same length as the back piece. Then cut 1⁄8" off each end to match the length of the lids.

TIP *I usually check wood carefully for cracks and splits that might cause problems in the finished piece. Sometimes, however, they will appear later, or the special character in the wood demands that a particular piece be used despite its flaws. Cracks and splits can be easy to fix. A business card with glue spread on both sides can be slipped into a crack, enabling glue to be spread in hard-to-reach places. Often a small chisel will be needed to widen the crack for the card to be inserted. When the card is pulled out, it will leave glue on both surfaces so the split can be clamped closed until the glue has set., and with modern adhesives, glued joints are often as strong as the wood itself.*

the stop block for drilling the opposite hole in the lid (photo 17). Drill the holes on the left, then the right, using the index piece to adjust the location of the stop block.

In order for the lid hinge holes to align with the holes in the back piece, the lengths of the tenons and the lid clearance must be allowed for. Move the fence on the drill press slightly more than ⅛", or use a ⅛" shim with a piece of paper or business card stock to provide for clearance. Forming a block, bring together the lid and the scrap saved from shaping the lid. Adjust the depth of the hole. You can drill deliberately under depth and then lower the depth by increments (photo 18). Drill another index piece so that the opposite hole can then be drilled without the shims and card stock.

To provide clearance for opening, rout a 45° chamfer on the back sides of the back and lid. Use a $\frac{1}{16}$" roundover bit to soften the top edge of the box front. If you wish to sand the inside of the box, do it now before the box is assembled.

Assemble the Box

Use a glue syringe for the mortises and areas where the box front and back will contact the ends (photo 19). Fit the front and back pieces to the bottom, and insert the tenons and panel ends into one box end first, then the other.

Insert the hinges into the box lid.

18 **I've stacked two lids face-to-face, eliminating the need to change the drill press table angle to conform with the sloping lid. I suggest using the scrap saved from shaping the lid earlier to form a square block to drill into.**

19 **Use a squeeze bottle to apply glue to the insides of the mortises, and assemble the box.**

20 **After the glue has set, tilt the band saw table to the same angle used for resawing the lids to trim away excess wood from the box ends. The ends should be nearly flush with the lid.**

21 **Use the stationary belt sander to sand the box ends flush with the ends, bottom and lid. Start with 100-grit and work down to 150 before moving to the orbital sander.**

22 **On the router table, shape the inside edge of the lid with a 1/16" roundover bit.**

The hinges are sometimes tight enough that no glue is required; however, if your hinges go in without much pressure, place a dab of glue in the hole. Position the lid, and insert the hinges in the back of the box, opening and closing the lid to check the clearance and that the box is square. Adjust the box by squeezing corner to corner if necessary.

Finish the Box

Set up the band saw at the same angle used for resawing the lid, but adjust the fence to allow for the width of the box. Pass the box between the fence and blade, trimming the excess material from the ends (photo 20).

For rough sanding, use the 6" × 48" belt sander with a coarse belt. Sand the ends flush with the top. Moving to finer grits, sand the top, front, back and bottom of the box (photo 21).

Open the box and, with the inside of the box lid against the fence, rout the inside edge of the lid with the 1/16" roundover bit (photo 22). After changing to a 1/8" roundover bit, rout all the edges of the box except for the front edge, which will be gently rounded as the box is orbital-sanded (photo 23).

Use the orbital sander to finish-sand the box, gently rolling the corners and edges. I start with 180-grit, then go to 240 and finally use 320-grit. Finish the box with Danish oil.

23 **After using a 1/8" roundover bit on all edges of the box, use the orbital sander to sand the surfaces smooth.**

Chapter 2

Triangle Ring Box

I enjoy figuring out new and simple ways to make things. It doesn't matter to me whether someone has done it before as long as I can have the pleasure of discovering it for myself. This ring box is made using a template and a simple jig to hold parts in place as a series of routing operations is performed. This same technique could be applied to a variety of shapes and sizes, and once the fixtures are made through a few simple steps, the box can easily be replicated in a variety of woods.

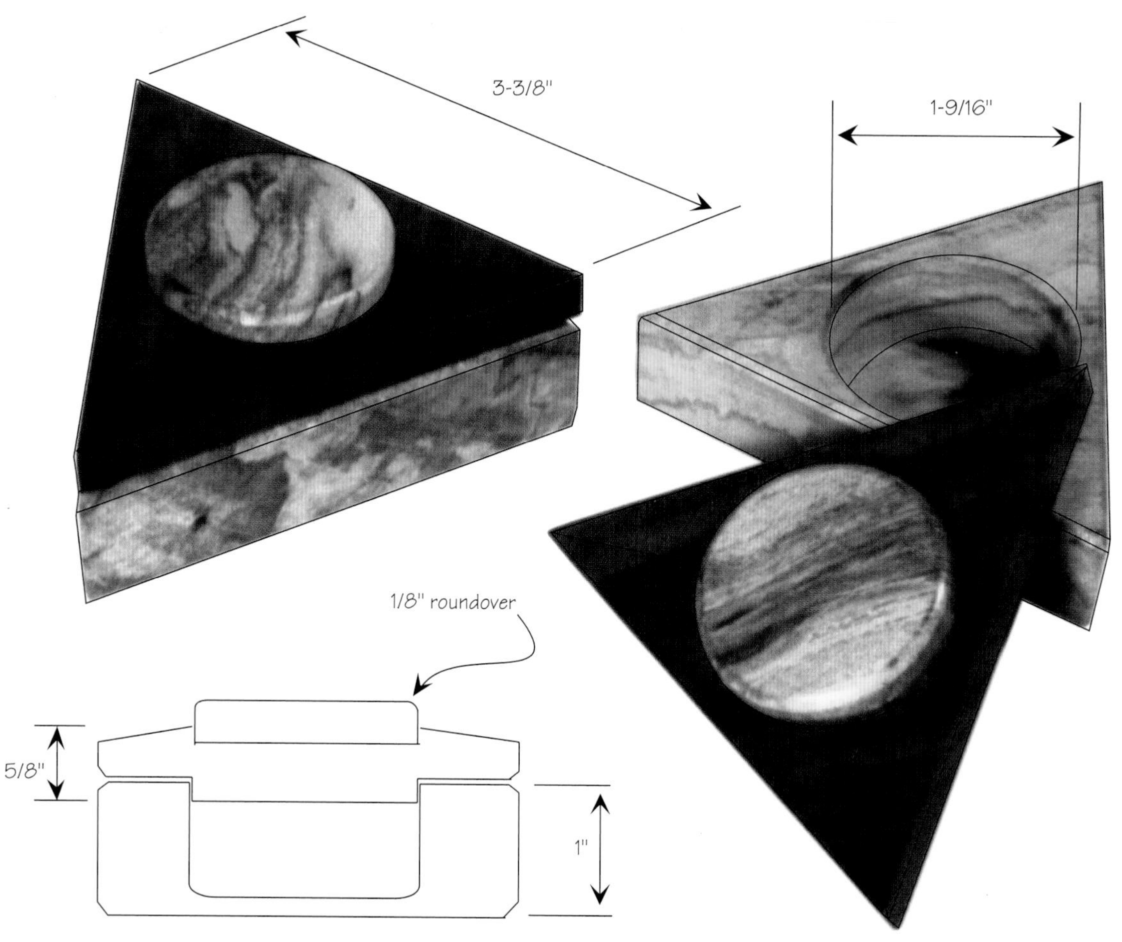

Bill of Materials

PART NAME	NUMBER	DIMENSION TWL	COMMENTS
Base	1	1" x 3⅜" each side	Cut from 3"-wide stock
Top	1	½" x 3⅜" each side	Cut from 3"-wide stock
Inlay	1	⅜" x 2" x 2"	Or larger

Router Platform and Template

PART NAME	NUMBER	DIMENSION TWL	COMMENTS
Platform	1	¾" x 8" x 11"	Plywood
Feet	2	¾" x 5" x 8"	Plywood
Template	1	¼" x 8" x 11"	Masonite or plywood
Dowels	4	¾" x 1¼"	Hardwood

Make the Routing Jig

This box uses a routing jig, a template-following router bit and an inlay routing set consisting of a ⅛" router bit and guide bushings. The templates are aligned with dowels that fit into holes drilled into the jig. This way the template can be removed for subsequent placement of parts. With imagination and a variety of layered templates, this technique can be expanded to make more complicated designs.

Make the Routing Platform

To allow you to clamp the platform to the bench without interfering with the jig, attach feet to the underside of the platform as shown in the photo. Drill ¾" holes in the corners of the platform for the dowels (photo 1).

The template stock should be tempered hardboard or Masonite. Cut the template to the same dimensions as the routing platform. Drill holes in the corners for screws in the same position as the ¾" holes in the routing platform (photo 2). Place ¾" dowels in the platform holes. Place the template piece on top, aligned with the corners, and attach the template to the dowels with wood screws. Countersink the screws so they won't interfere with the movement of the router.

Make the Triangle Ring Box

By simply changing router bits, a single template is used for the interior shape, the lip of the lid, the space for the inlay and the inlay itself.

Make the Box Base

To cut the triangle shapes with the table saw, use a sliding table or sled and a temporary tack-in-place fence to set the angle of cut (photos 3, 4).

In the center of the template board, drill a hole about ¼" larger in diameter than the size desired for the interior of the box (photo 5).

Trace the hole onto the router platform so that it lines up with the hole in the template, then pencil the position of the triangle around the circle (photo 6). Place the triangle piece over the circle, and attach blocking to hold the

1 **Clamp the routing platform to the workbench. The holes provide for accurate alignment of the layered templates.**

2 **Screw through the template stock into hardwood dowels, so the template will be easy to remove and replace over the workpiece.**

3 **Tack a temporary fence to the table saw sled when cutting the body of the ring box.**

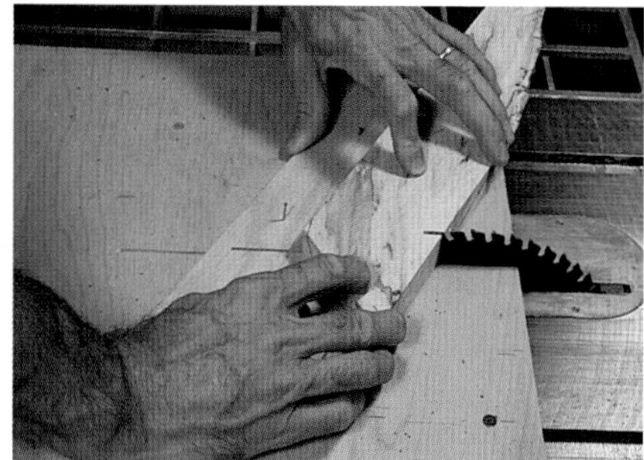

4 Use the sled to cut the box bodies and lids to equal size.

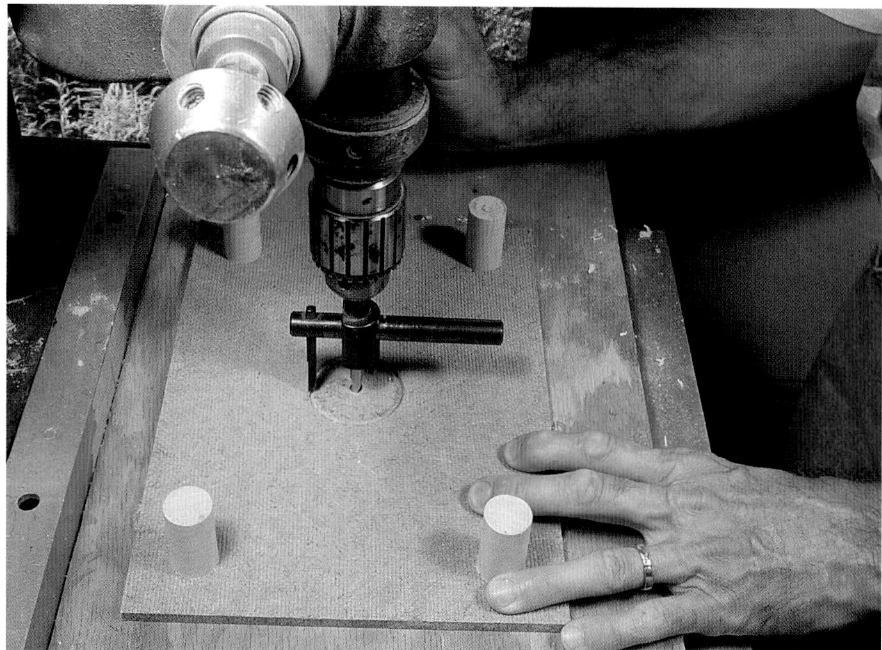

5 Drill a large hole in the center of the template stock to use as a guide for shaping the interior space and the lid, as well as making and fitting the inlay.

6 Trace the circle from the template onto the routing platform, and then lay out the position of the box body in pencil.

triangle in place (photo 7).

Over the triangle piece, set the template onto the platform. With a ⅛" bit cutter and an inlay guide bushing with brass bushing mounted on it, rout the circle into the top of the triangle piece. Rout to a depth of at least ⅛" (photo 8). This will outline the shape of the box interior, providing a guide surface for the next step.

Insert a bowl-cutting bit or dado bit into your plunge router. Remove the waste inside the box base to form the interior space (photo 9). A standard router can be used but will require frequent depth changes. The cut must be made deep enough for the bearing to contact the edge defined in the earlier operation before routing the outside portion of the interior space.

7 Position stop blocks around the box body to hold it in place. Attach the stop blocks to the routing platform with brads or screws.

8 Use the router inlay set to begin routing the inside shape of the box. This should be done with the brass bushing in place. Rout only about ⅛" deep, forming a lip that will be followed to form the inside of the box.

9 Use the bowl-cutting bit with the guide bearing in the plunge router to continue forming the inside of the box. Lower the cutter gradually into the center of the box and move toward the sides until the bearing contacts the edge formed by the inlay router set. Make the cut in several steps, taking time between steps to remove waste.

Make the Lid

Remove the box base from the guide blocks, and put the lid in its place, bottom facing up. Before routing, apply a layer of tape to the inside edge of the template. This will keep the lid from fitting too tightly. Remove the brass bushing from the guide bushing set and with the ⅛" router bit, rout the perimeter of the template (photo 10). Be careful to hold the guide bushing against the edge of the template.

Remove the template; this routing operation will be performed freehand. To provide router support, arrange wood pieces of the same thickness as the lid around the guide blocks. With a straight-cut bit adjusted to match the depth of cut on the lip, rout away the waste stock at the three corners (photo 11). Use a small chisel to clean up the cut (photo 12).

10 To rout the lip on the lid, remove the brass bushing. With the lid held in the router platform, lower the router into the template. Hold the guide bushing firmly to one side.

11 To remove the additional waste around the lip, remove the template. Arrange pieces of the same thickness as the lid to support the router. Cut toward the lip as you control the router freehand.

12 If needed, use a small chisel to clean up the cut.

Inlay the Lid

Turn the lid over, exposing the top, and replace the template. With the guide bushing and brass bushing in place, rout the recess for the inlay piece to fit into. Rout to a ⅛" depth, moving in circles to remove all the waste stock within the space defined by the template.

Place some inlay stock in the template assembly. It will help if the inlay stock is cut to fit tightly within the holding blocks on the routing platform. Place double-stick carpet tape on the bottom of the inlay piece to keep it from moving. Remove the brass bushing from the guide bushing, and lower the depth of cut on the router bit so it equals the thickness of the inlay stock (photo 13). Hold the guide bushing against the side of the template, gently lowering the router bit into the stock.

WORKING WITH "REAL" WOOD

A note of caution: When one gets to the scale of box where a small lid opens and closes to tight tolerances, a woodworker enters the realm where 1/64" or less can make a difference in the look or feel of a thing. We must put aside the tools of measurement and test the fit of the actual parts as the project grows and evolves toward completion. The dimensions offered in these chapters are "starting points." It could be a mistake to begin making one of these boxes by cutting all the parts to size.

Using "real" wood adds to the complications. Solid hardwoods continue to breathe, responding to ambient humidity changes in the environment. Dimensions change. What was flat may cup and curl. It's a darn hard thing to reconcile with a person's woodworking aspirations.

I have a personal inclination toward working with "difficult" woods that come with a history attached. They may have grown up in a neighbor's yard or come "air-dried" from lumberyards where storage conditions were less than ideal. Many of these woods would not be available from normal hardwood dealers, but I like working with these woods. They bring a quality of adventure to my work. They often challenge my self-esteem when things don't work out quite as I expect. It helps to have a go-with-the-flow attitude, to remember not to take myself too seriously. Woodworking is about having fun, right?

Following the template, free the inlay piece from the surrounding material.

Shape the Lid and Base

With the table saw blade at a 10° angle, cut the top to shape (photo 14).

Rout the edges of the base and the underside of the lid with a chamfering bit on the router table. This requires changing the height of cut above the router table for the various parts. I prefer a larger cut at the bottom of the box and very small chamfered edges where the lid meets the base. Rout the top of the inlay piece with a roundover bit prior to gluing it in the box top.

Sand all parts prior to assembly.

13 Remove the brass bushing; rout the inlay piece to fit. Hold the router tightly to the perimeter of the hole in the template. Double-stick carpet tape will hold the center piece in place.

14 Use the table saw to shape the lid, adding interest to the finished box. Sand away the saw marks with a sanding block.

With the lid in place on the box base, start the sanding operation on the belt and disc sander; then use the orbital sander for the finer grits. The chamfers will be best sanded with a sanding block to avoid rounding.

Chapter 3

Lathe-Turned Ring Box

My lathe-turned ring boxes are a way that I make use of the mixed hardwood scraps from my custom furniture making. The material costs me nothing but the inconvenience of having too much clutter in my shop. I seldom stick too closely to plans in my turning, preferring to enjoy the creative play as refined shapes emerge from blocks of wood. You may find, as I did, that making just one design is not enough.

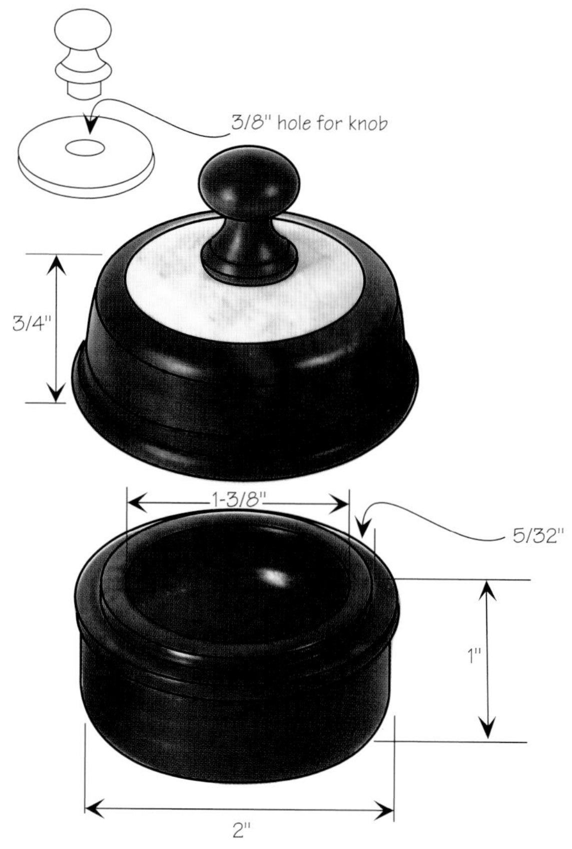

Bill of Materials

PART NAME	NUMBER	DIMENSION TWL	COMMENTS
Base	1		Cut from 2½" x 9" stock
Lid	1		Cut from 2½" x 9" stock
Pull	1		Turned from ⅝"-square stock
Inlay	1	⅛" x 2" x 2"	

With the lathe-turned ring box, the design possibilities are limitless.

A Note About Tools

I use my 1948 model 10 ER Shopsmith lathe and a SuperNova chuck with pin-chuck jaws. The SuperNova chuck is designed to lock tightly into a dovetailed recess cut into the workpiece. The recess gives a completed foot to the work without leaving any obvious point of attachment. It also facilitates accurate realignment if the piece needs to go back on the lathe to adjust the fit of the lid. A simple template and dovetail bit are needed to rout the recess in the bottom. Any bit of scrap with one flat side and that is large enough for the dovetailed recess is fair game for turning.

Making the Box

Select a piece of 2½" × 9" stock from your scrap pile. I prefer fine-textured woods like maple, walnut or persimmon, but sometimes coarser woods like oak or chinkapin can provide interesting contrast. The pieces for the top and bottom need not be the same size, thickness or species of wood. If the stock does not have a flat side, and is not large enough to safely pass across the jointer, use the 6" × 48" belt sander to sand a flat spot. For turning the pull, smaller square stock can be used. For the inlay, band saw a ⅛"-thick slice from a scrap of wood of contrasting color.

To make the template, use ⅛" or ¼" plywood or hardboard Masonite. I make my template large enough to allow clamps to hold it in place without interfering with the router. As an option, a smaller template can be held in place with screws. On the drill press, drill a 1¼" hole in the hardboard. The hole need not be precisely 1¼" (photo 1).

Clamp the template in place, and rout the dovetailed recesses in the base and lid. Use a 7⁄16" guide bushing and a 5⁄16" dovetail bit to rout the recess to a depth of approximately ⅛". Rout the back of another scrap piece for use as a mini faceplate for shaping the inlay. This piece should be surfaced uniformly on both sides. It can be solid stock, ¾" particleboard or plywood.

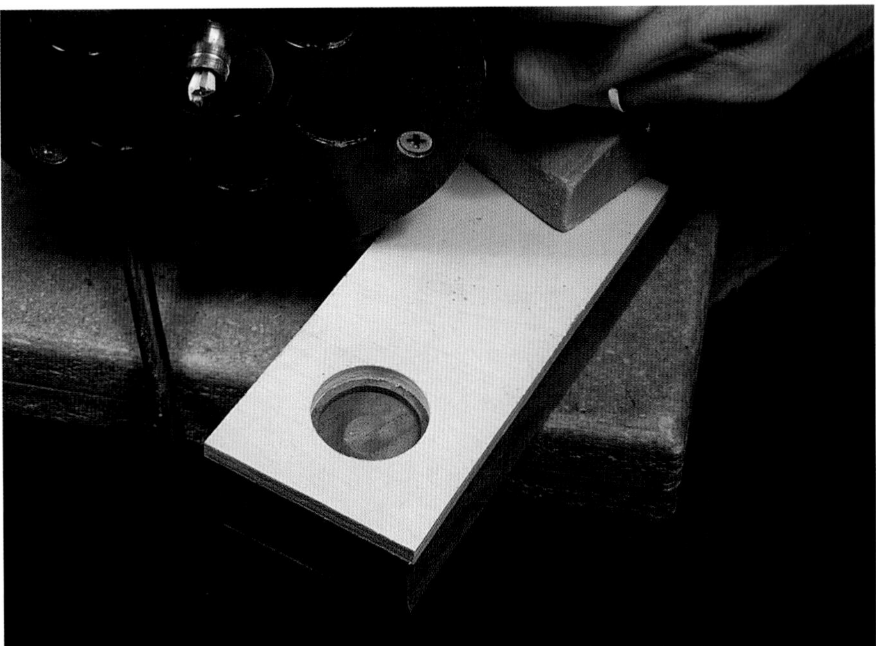

1 Drill a 1¼" hole in scrap plywood to form the template for routing dovetail recesses. The template will be clamped to the hardwood stock.

2 On the lathe, shape the inside of the base. Use a skew chisel to form the lip that will hold the lid in place.

Shape the Body of the Box

To make the stock easier to shape on the lathe, cut off the corners with your band saw. Mount the bottom stock in the chuck. Using a small gouge, hollow out the inside of the box. Make a dovetail recess in the first ⅜" to ½" of the opening so that when the box is reversed in the chuck, the dovetailed jaws will grip securely. The opening must be carefully planned to not cut through into the recess on the bottom. Using a skew, cut the shape of the box lip to fit the planned overlap of the lid. Use various lathe tools to shape the upper area of the box bottom (photo 2). Sand the interior, lip and top surfaces of the base with a succession of sanding grits.

Remove the base from the chuck,

3 Turn over the base, and reattach it to the lathe chuck. The slight dovetail recess you left on the inside of the base will allow the chuck to hold it tightly. Use the gouge to shape the bottom of the box.

4 Sand the base while it is on the lathe. Progress from 150-grit through 320-grit.

5 Use calipers to gauge the box lid as it is formed; first the inside shape, and then after the box is turned over in the chuck, the space for the inlay to fit.

and turn it over so the chuck will be able to tighten inside the opening of the box. Check to make sure that the box is on evenly and securely. Use the gouge to shape the lower portion of the box bottom, then sand (photos 3, 4).

Make the Inlay

I use a piece of sugar maple with a dovetail recess cut into the back to hold it to the lathe as a mini faceplate. Attach the ⅛"-thick veneer inlay to the mini faceplate with double-stick carpet tape. Mount the mini faceplate in the chuck, and cut the inlay piece to size with the skew (photo 5).

To shape the inside of the lid, repeat the sequence used for the base. Once again, the opening must widen, forming a dovetail shape, in order for the chuck to fit. Use calipers to make sure the size of the opening conforms to that of the bottom (photo 6). Use the skew to cut the lip wider so the base will fit the lid.

Remove the lid from the chuck and remount it with the chuck gripping the inside. Use the gouge to form the shape of the lid. Then use the skew to form and adjust the recess for the inlay to fit into. Carefully glue the inlay in place (photo 7). With the inlay in place, use the skew to level the inlay with the surrounding wood. Sand the lid and, using

Leaving a Legacy in Wood

My uncle Ron Stowe passed away in October 1997 at the age of 89. As a woodworker, I will always derive inspiration from my memories of him and from his legacy in wood.

He began wood turning at the age of seventy. He took classes and enthusiastically embraced the technical expertise of his teachers. His first work, a mimosa candle stand, closely resembled a two-pound coffee can, but he improved rapidly and steadily. He grew toward an aesthetic vision and a technical proficiency that would allow his work to be sold in galleries in Louisiana and Texas.

When he found himself producing work at a pace faster than the galleries could sell, he would save some of it for distribution at the biannual Stowe family reunions. He often brought over 150 pieces. To decide the order for choosing their favorites, family members drew numbers from a spalted maple bowl. The youngest were never excluded, often allowed to go first.

My uncle Ron and his legacy in wood have helped me to better understand the opportunity we have as woodworkers to make this world a better place. I cherish his memory, both for the encouragement he offered and for the example he set.

the skew chisel, cut the hole in the top for the pull to fit into.

Make the Pull

Cut ½"-square stock to a 4" length. Mount the stock, using the SuperNova chuck as a pin chuck, and turn it to a pleasing shape. To cut the shape, use a small gouge and the skew chisel. Use the parting tool to form the tenon for the pull to fit in the lid (photo 8). Check the size with calipers.

On the lathe, sand the pull through a range of grits. Start at 100-grit, and finish at 320. Finally, leaving enough of the tenon to fit the lid, use the skew chisel to cut the pull from the remaining stock.

Glue the pull in place, and use a wiping varnish or Danish oil to bring the colors of the woods to life.

6 Use inside calipers to check that the interior space in the lid matches that of the base.

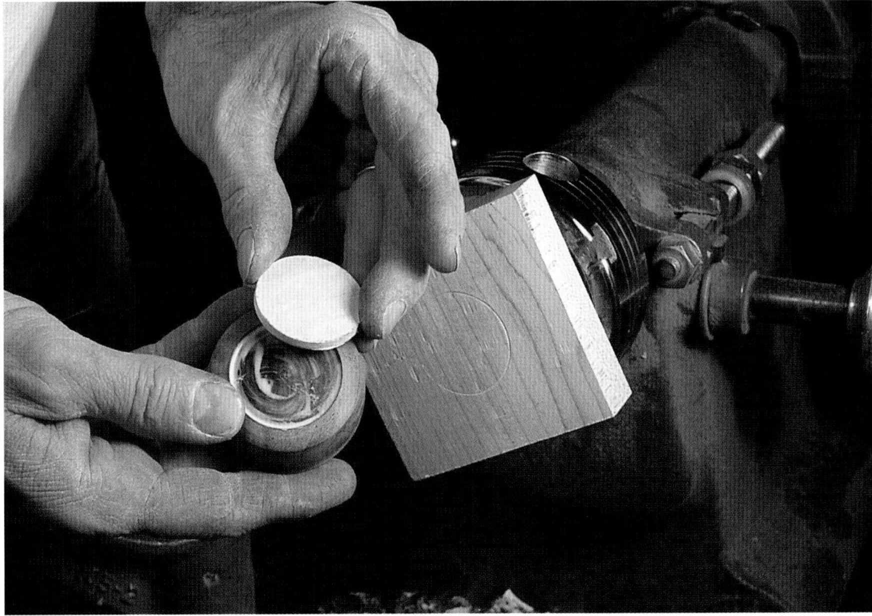

7 Spread glue on the inside of the recess cut in the top surface of the lid and press the inlay piece in place. After the inlay is glued in place, the lid can be put back on the lathe for final shaping and to cut the hole for the pull to fit.

8 Shape the pull. Use your imagination to create something that contributes to the overall design of the box.

Chapter 4

Half-Turned Box

This box, with its soft, feminine curves, is perfect for presenting a string of pearls or for storing small treasures. Each box is half of a complete turned form, made more interesting by the way it presents a profile of the turned shape. I made my boxes from cherry, walnut and sassafras, turning the boxes on the lathe, two lids at a time. The interior shape of the base is created using a bowl-cutting router bit with a bearing mounted on the shaft, following a template cut out on the scroll saw.

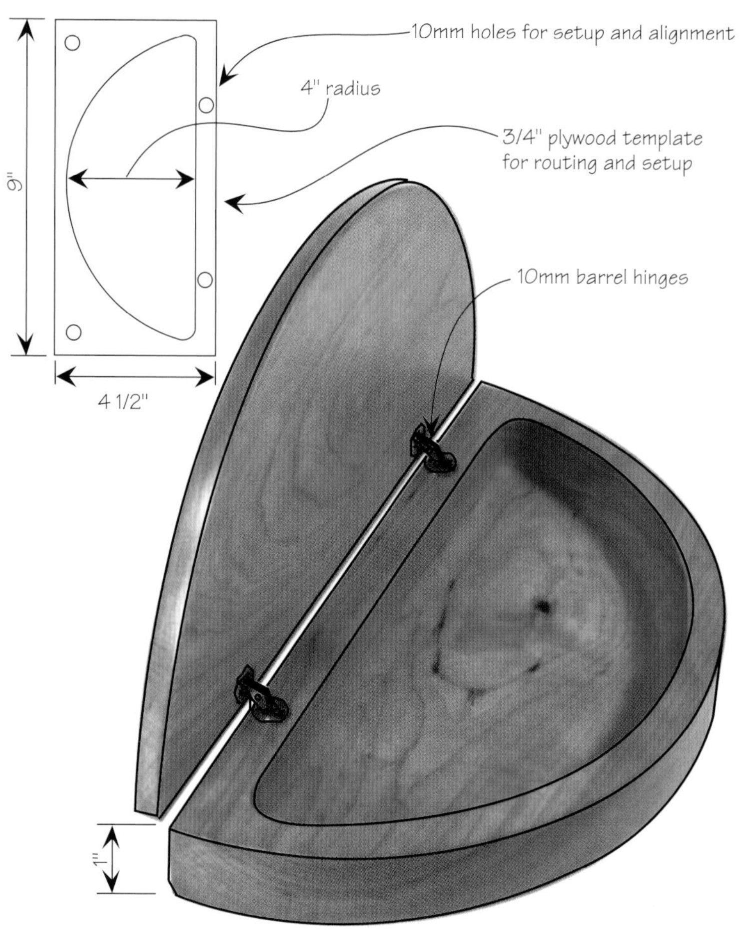

Bill of Materials

PART NAME	NUMBER	DIMENSION TWL	COMMENTS
Bases	2	1" x 4½" x 9"	
Lids	2	1" x 4½" x 9"	

Hardware

10mm Barrel Hinges (2 pr)

1 **Use stops clamped on the drill press fence to position the holes for indexing the workpieces to the faceplate assembly. The 10mm drill is sized to fit the 10mm barrel hinges that will attach the lid to the base of the box. Use the same setup to drill the matching holes for the template.**

Making the Faceplate Assembly and Template

Cut two pieces of ¾" plywood to size: one exactly square, the other exactly half the width of the larger one. The square piece will become the wood faceplate. The smaller rectangular piece will become the template for routing the base and drilling the hinge holes.

Find the center point of the wood faceplate, marking from corner to corner with a pencil. This point will be used when drilling, to align the wood to the cast-iron faceplate of your lathe. Using the dimensions in the template diagram, mark out the holes for the dowels that will fit the hinge holes, and hold the lids to the faceplate assembly. For this technique to be safe and efficient, the wood has to be sound, without splits or cracks that could allow the wood to separate from the faceplate assembly. If you're uncertain about the soundness, an additional screw can be used through the faceplate, firmly anchoring the wood. This is also a good option if you're unsure of your ability to turn the wood without digging in too abruptly with the lathe chisels.

On the drill press, drill 10mm holes into the wooden faceplate and template. Use a stop block to align the holes in both pieces. Drill an index piece to help in setting up to drill the opposite holes. Open the hinge, and measure the distance between the barrels to determine the clearance required (see photo 1).

2 **By drilling a hole the same size as the lathe arbor at the center of the wooden faceplate, accurate alignment to the cast-iron faceplate can be achieved.**

To attach the faceplate, first drill a hole the same size as the lathe arbor at the center point of the faceplate block. Slip the faceplate block over the arbor of the lathe, then the faceplate. Using the arbor to assure their alignment, use screws to attach the faceplate block to the faceplate (see photo 2). If your lathe has a Morse taper faceplate attachment, you must align the parts by careful measuring. Then, the faceplate assembly can be removed, reversed, and firmly attached to the lathe with

3 Assemble the wood faceplate to the cast-iron faceplate by putting them on the lathe arbor in reverse order.

4 Use a straight-cut router bit to begin defining the interior space for the template, moving the template piece between stops along the router table fence. Note the pencil sketch showing the planned interior space. As you move the workpiece back and forth, gradually raise the cutter until it penetrates through the top. Another option is to turn the piece over, end for end, between raising the router bit, and stopping when the cuts join.

5 Use the scroll saw to further define the interior space.

lightly sanded ⅜" dowels that fit into the 10mm holes. Taper the ends of the dowels slightly so the lids can be removed after turning (see photo 3).

Rout the Template

Use the router table and a straight-cut bit to form the back inside edge of the template. Use stops to control the movement along the fence, and raise the router bit in increments until it penetrates through the template. To reduce the number of steps in raising the cutter, and to leave the router bit safely buried in wood until the final cut, cut in on one side of the template and then the other, finally having the two cuts meet at the center (see photo 4).

Define the Box Interior

Use a scroll saw to define the interior space of the box. The interior space can echo the exterior shape, or can be free-form to offer a surprise. Use a

6 Smooth the interior space in the template using a rotary or handheld rasp, a small sanding drum or coarse sandpaper.

7 Use the 10mm hinge holes to set up the stops and fence on the drill press for the hinge/indexing holes in the lid and base parts. You may set up to drill one end and then move the stop to drill the other, or set up two stops to control drilling the matching holes.

8 Drill the 10mm holes into the lid and base parts, changing the location of the stop for drilling the opposite hole. Check the depth of the hole with your dial caliper, making certain the depth is equal to half the total length of the barrel hinge.

sanding drum or small grinder in the drill press to clean up the interior shape of the template (see photos 5, 6).

Turn the Lids

First, cut the lid and base parts to dimension. Each part should be the same finished size as the template. Then use the template to set up stops on the drill press, and to set the position of the fence. Set the drill to penetrate half the length of the closed barrel hinge (see photo 7). If the tops and bottoms are the same thickness, they can be drilled with the same setup. Use a dial caliper to check the depth. Then, drill the hinge holes for the tops and bottoms of the boxes (see photo 8).

Squeeze the box tops into place on the faceplate assembly and, after trimming to shape on the band saw (see photo 9), mount it on the lathe. As you work, remember the locations of the hinge holes, and avoid cutting too deep

9 Use double-stick carpet tape and 3/8" dowels to attach the lids to the faceplate. The 3/8" dowels will need to be sanded smaller to fit in the 10mm holes. Before turning the lids on the lathe, use the band saw to cut away most of the waste, providing a nearly round turning blank.

10 Use a variety of lathe tools to shape the lids. Remember the locations and depth of the hinge holes to avoid cutting through the lids.

On the Meaning of Recreation

I subscribe to the rec.woodworking newsgroup on the Internet. It gives me the opportunity to communicate with other woodworkers, sharing some of what I have learned, learning from their experience and enthusiasm. It is a group of mainly amateur woodworkers. The *rec* in the title refers to recreation, but even a "professional" woodworker like me can find kindred spirits there. To recreate means to restore, refresh, create anew, to put fresh life into; refresh or restore in body or mind, especially after work, by some form of play, amusement or relaxation. Recreation is more than just having something to do after work. The time we spend daydreaming, planning, browsing through the latest catalogs, hanging out in the newsgroup and working in the shop is time for renewal and restoration of spirit. Whether our hard work creates something to show is beside the point. The hidden object of our pursuit is the re-creation of ourselves.

A friend of mine, Joe, is married to an outspoken and vivacious woman who grew up in a family with very sophisticated tastes. When he completed his first and only attempt at woodworking, an entertainment center made from pine, it didn't come close to resembling anything that Babs could call furniture. You can imagine the scene: Joe basking in the delight of accomplishment, and Babs, not being one to miss the opportunity to say what's on her mind, lets it rip. Joe's foray into the world of recreational woodworking ground to a screeching halt. This happened several years ago. The entertainment center was cut into kindling and went up in smoke along with the last of Joe's woodworking aspirations. There is still a touch of pain in his voice when he describes his only woodworking adventure.

There are two woodworkings, the first being the idealized one, the woodworking of expectations, where everything turns out perfect. The spouse is pleased, each and every joint is of Krenovian perfection, and we are exalted on the shoulders of our peers. Then there is the real thing, the nitty-gritty. It consists of wood putty, not enough clamps, the desperate need for a lumber stretcher, and all the questions asked in the newsgroup when the confidence of "Yes! I can do that!" meets the reality of "*Oops!*"

This separation between expectation and reality was what happened to woodworking when "Eve ate the apple and discovered she needed furniture." Mankind was thrust from heavenly pleasure in the process of woodworking into the real world of having to create something measurable to show for it.

So I try to keep things in perspective: We are all "newbies" at something. Our encouragement of each other is essential. The best woodworking experiences are the ones that bring us humility, understanding and personal growth. Our best work comes from our willingness to take chances and risk failure. Perfection exists only as an objective to be reached toward. And moment-by-moment satisfaction from the process of woodworking is the best reward. So, have fun! Tune in to rec.woodworking! Share what you've learned with others! If you find Joe out there in the world, invite him to your shop and get him started with something smaller than an entertainment center. How about a box?

11 To connect the template to the box base stock, use ⅜" dowels sanded to fit the 10mm holes. With a bowl-cutting bit and guide bearing mounted on the router bit shaft, use a plunge router to gradually cut away the interior of the box. After roughing out most of the interior, rout in very small circular patterns to smooth the bottom to make it uniform.

in those areas. No exact shape is required, so this is a good time to play until you find an interesting one (see photo 10).

Sand the lid smooth, starting with 100-grit, then 180, 240 and finally 320-grit. Then pry the finished lids from the faceplate assembly.

Make the Base

Insert short dowels into the holes on the template to hold it securely to the box bottom. Use a plunge router and a template-following bowl bit to hollow out the space. Gradually lower the cutter in small increments, taking time between operations to remove accumulated router dust. When you reach the bottom of the planned cut, move the router in small circles to flatten the bottom (see photo 11).

Remove the template and, using ⅜" dowels, press the lid and base together (see photo 12). Use the band saw to cut the outline of the box bottom to rough shape and, with either a sander disc in your table saw or a belt/disc sander, sand the edges even (see photo 13).

Finally, soften the edges where the boxes open and close with a 1/16" roundover bit in the router table. Sand the inside of the lid and the top of the base with the orbital sander. Install the hinges before sanding the back and front edges of the box. Finish the box with three coats of Danish oil.

12 Alignment pins placed in the hinge holes attach the lid and base for final shaping. You can band saw the bottom shape to conform to the lid or use your imagination.

13 If you wish to make the lid conform to the base, a sanding disc in the table saw will sand them flush. A very light touch is required to avoid damaging your hard work.

Chapter 5

Bracelet Box

One of my favorite boxes from my earlier book, Creating Beautiful Boxes With Inlay Techniques, *was the tea box. The tea box had a crotch-figured walnut top, "locked" or finger-jointed corners and a narrow inlay band of cherry and maple. This box is another offering of that beautiful combination. The crotch figure is formed where major limbs intersect, giving an intense multidirectional grain pattern that is dense and highly reflective. Crotch-figured walnut is very heavy, difficult to work and among the most beautiful of woods. It is also very common. I often have pieces of crotch-figured walnut left over from furniture making where its tendency to be less stable is a disadvantage, and where its striking figure is hard to use. Crotch-figured walnut is most commonly available in low-grade lumber, making it a special reward for the bargain hunter willing to dig through the woodpile.*

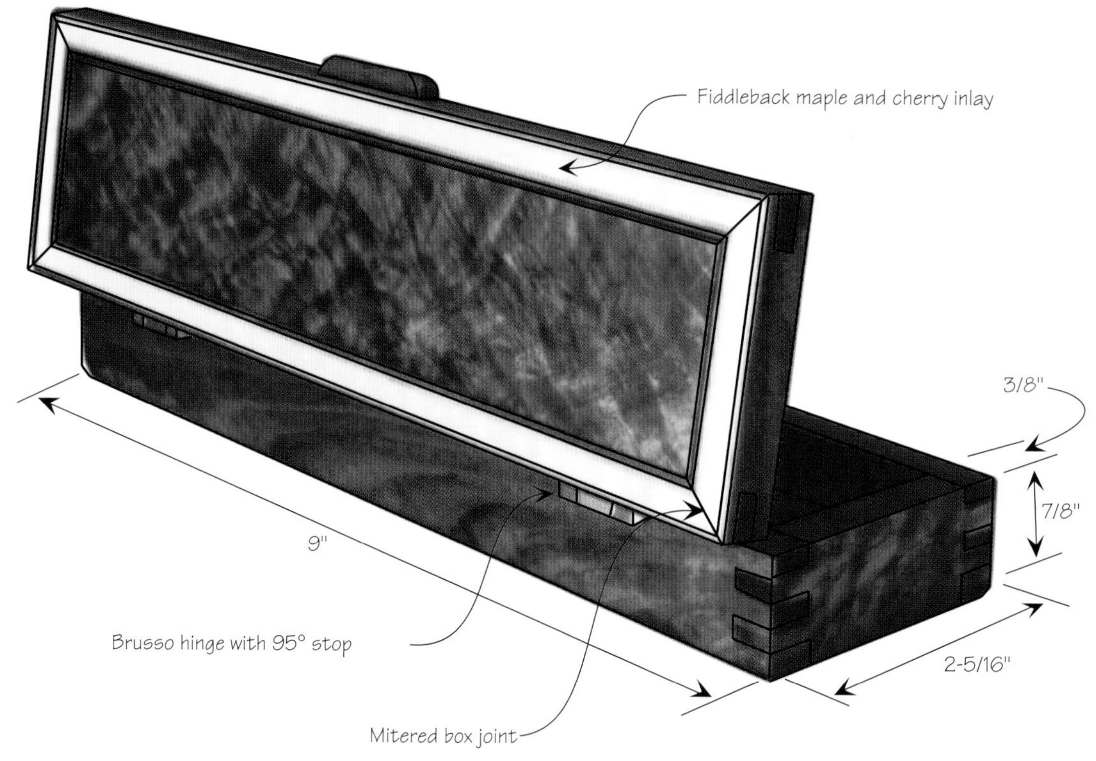

Bill of Materials

PART NAME	NUMBER	DIMENSION TWL	COMMENTS
Ends	2	3/8 x 1 1/2 x 2 5/16	
Front	1	3/8 x 1 1/2 x 9	
Back	2	3/8 x 1 1/2 x 9	
Top	1	3/8 x 1 1/2 x 8 7/16	
Bottom	1	1/8 x 1 1/2 x 8 7/16	Baltic birch plywood

Hardware

3/4" Brusso Solid Brass Hinges With Built-in Stop (1 pr.)

Prepare the Stock

Resaw the walnut into thin panels for the top and sides on the band saw. Use the most highly figured walnut for the top panel. Crotch walnut is prone to warping, so flatten one side on the jointer before ripping. After ripping, plane it down with the planer. A thickness sander is helpful in bringing crotch walnut to final thickness because crotch walnut has a tendency to tear out in planing. The side panels can be book-matched to bring continuous grain around the box.

Make the Inlay

Making inlay bands requires a great deal of accuracy in milling the thickness of parts. I have found that thin parts can more easily be sanded to dimension than planed. This is because when stock gets very thin, it may lift into the planer knives, giving an uneven thickness. Sanding exerts a more even pressure against the stock, allowing more accurate dimensions to be achieved. I often use a drum sander to "thickness" stock, particularly when it is very thin, or highly figured and prone to tear out during planing. A disc sander for the table saw is a good alternative.

Rip thin strips of maple and cherry. Use the disc sander to sand the parts

Making A Box Joint Jig

This box joint jig looks complicated but is fairly easy to make. The sliding work table and base to which the router is attached are cut from a single piece of 3/4" plywood. The dadoes for the hardwood runners to fit are cut before the plywood is cut into the two sections of the jig. There are no exact dimensions required for making an effective jig. After cutting the two sections from the plywood, an additional dado is required to attach the fence to the sliding table. I used hard maple to make the runners for my jig. They need to be carefully planed to fit: tight enough to give good control, but loose enough to slide easily. This will take a bit of careful trial and error. Use screws to attach the router base to the bottom of the jig, counter sinking the screws to be flush with the top of the jig base., and wood screws to attach the sliding runners to the jig base.

After attaching the router to the base, use a straight cut router bit to cut though the base to provide clearance for the bit and collet. This is done with the upper section out of the way, and by gradually raising the router in a series of cuts. Next, put the upper section in place. With the 3/16" router bit installed in the router, gradually raise the bit while sliding the upper section of the jig over the cutter. This will open up the clearance for the router bit to pass. You may find it

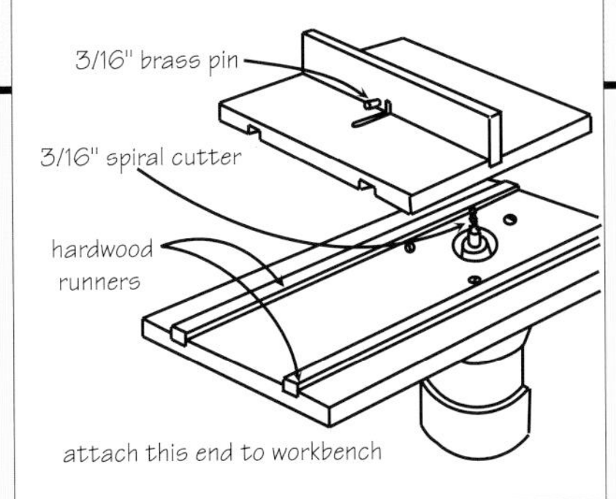

necessary to route additional clearance with a larger router bit for the 3/16" bit to raise high enough through the sliding table. Use hardwood to make the fence for the jig. I used a 3/16" brass pin to form the stop which controls the position of the work-piece. Drill a hole for the pin to fit before installing the fence on the sliding table. Its location should be 3/16" from the router's line of cut. Use wood screws to attach the fence to the sliding table.

If you are very lucky, the jig will cut perfect box joints the first try. Normally, however, a bit of finessing will be required. To fine tune the jig for a perfect fit, remove the screws holding the fence to the sliding table and bump it over very slightly to compensate for fingers being too tight or too loose. With the jig viewed from the angle shown in the drawing, moving the fence to the left will tighten the fit of the fingers. Moving the fence to the right will make them loose.

1 Use the tapered sanding disc in the table saw to "thickness" the inlay strip.

2 Rout the channel for the inlay to fit.

3 Spread glue in the routed channel.

4 Press the inlay into the routed channel.

5 Clamp the parts edge to edge while the glue dries.

6 Make your first cut on a piece of scrap, then turn it over and clamp it to the box-joint jig. This will position the box ends for the first cuts.

to thickness, and then glue them together. I use thick hardwood backing blocks to make certain that the glued-up strip is flat.

Sand both sides of the inlay block on the disc sander, adjusting the fence to bring the block to the desired thickness (see photo 1). Use the dial caliper to check that the dimensions are the same on both sides. If not, adjust the angle of the disc. Try to remove equal amounts from both sides of the block so that the maple will have equal cherry borders. Then, using the thin-kerf blade in the table saw, rip 3⁄32"-thick inlay strips from the block.

Inlay the Sides

Cut the box parts to length. With a ¼" straight-cut router bit in the router table, rout the channels for inlay strips to fit into. Be sure to adjust the fence to place the channels at the centers of the box parts (see photo 2). If the fit is not perfect on the first try, widen the space between the cutter and fence very slightly and rout the parts again.

Cut the inlay strips to the required lengths. Spread glue in the channels, and press the inlays in place (see photos 3, 4). Arrange the box sides in pairs, and clamp them edge to edge to make sure pressure is evenly distributed to the inlay (see photo 5).

7 Proceed with the balance of the cuts on the ends, front and back.

8 Note the completed front piece with stock remaining for the mitered corner.

9 Use the miter sled to trim the miters on the ends and the front and back pieces. A stop block controls the position of the cut.

10 To cut the miters on the front and back parts, make sure the blade height equals the thickness of the remaining fingers on the box ends. Make a series of cuts sliding the workpiece in toward the stop. Note the finished miter joint.

Finger Joint the Corners

To cut the finger joints, I use a shop-made router jig and a spiral cutter. The spiral cutter reduces tear-out and gives more accurate cuts.

Push a piece of scrap stock against the alignment pin, and make a through cut. Then, with the scrap piece reversed, clamp it in place on the box-joint jig fence (see photo 6).

With the scrap guide piece in place, make the first cuts in the end pieces. The bottom edges must be pushed up tightly to the guide piece. After the first cuts are made, remove the guide piece and make the remaining cuts, lifting the stock over the guide pin for each successive cut (see photo 7). Cut the fingers in the front and back parts of the box, stopping short of the final cut to allow for the mitered corners at the top of the box (see photo 8).

Miter the Corners

I believe mitered joints on finger-jointed boxes give a more finished look, and they allow the use of inlay banding.

Use the table saw and sled to cut the miters on the box ends. The mitered cut on the inside of the box must align with the depth of the finger slots. This tends to be a trial-and-error process. A stop block clamped to the fence allows the cut to be changed in very small increments. Set the height of cut at just barely the amount required to cut through the fingers on the box ends. The same setting can be used for mitering the front and back

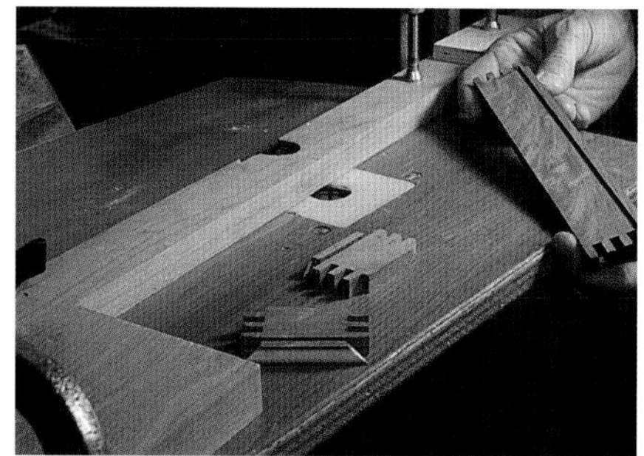

11 Rout for the top and bottom to fit. The stops on the fence prevent the dado from appearing on the outside of the box.

12 Use a squeeze bottle to apply the glue carefully to the fingers as you assemble the box around the top and bottom.

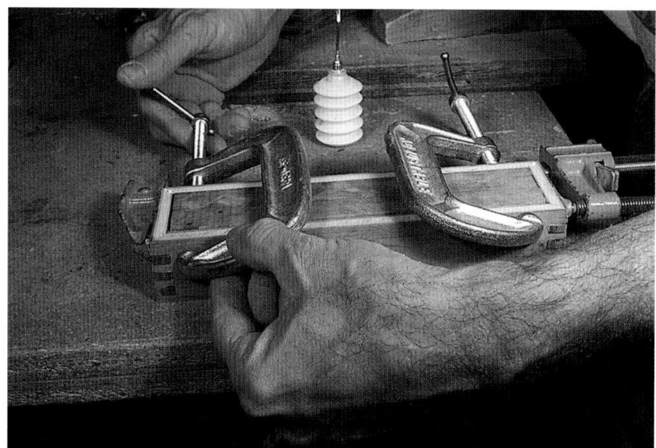

13 Clamp the box parts in position while the glue dries.

14 Use the tapered sanding disc in the table saw to shape the top of the box. The arbor is tilted to facet the top of the box. I shape my boxes by moving the fence toward the disc in three steps.

pieces (see photos 9, 10).

Reverse the angle of the fence, and cut the opposite sides. Once again, this is a trial-and-error operation. Check the fit of the box ends to the front or back to see that the miter closes tightly. Use a straight chisel to clean up the cuts.

Make the Top and Bottom Panels

Set up stops on the router table fence to control the length of cut. Using a ⅛" straight-cut bit, rout the dadoes for the top and bottom panels to fit the sides. To keep the dado invisible from outside the box, use the fence stops to restrict the length of the dado (see photo 11).

Use a 1" straight-cut bit in the router table to form the tongues on the top panel to fit the dadoes in all four sides. For the heavily figured walnut, I make relief cuts with the table saw to ease the router's work and to make it easier to control the workpiece. Check the fit of the top panel in the dadoes.

Cut the bottom panel to size and check its fit in the dadoes. If it's too tight, use the same setup on the router table to cut the edges of the panel to fit.

Assemble the Box

Sand the inside of the box. Then use a glue syringe to apply glue to the surfaces of the fingers (see photo 12). Put the top panel and bottom in place, and assemble the box parts.

Carefully observe to make sure the miters pull tightly together. The space around the top panel should be even all around. Clamp the box tightly together while the glue dries (see photo 13).

15 To cut the lid loose from the base, set the band saw fence so that the blade will cut at the joint between fingers.

16 With a 1/8" straight-cut bit in the router table, form the mortise for the lid tab to fit. Stop blocks are used to control the length of cut.

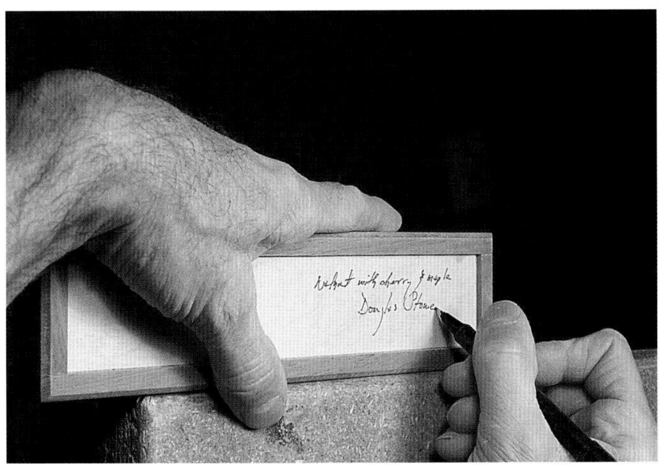

17 In signing my work, I like to give acknowledgment to the woods used.

18 The application of an oil finish brings beautiful wood to life. This is one of my favorite parts of the process.

Finish the Box

Use the belt and disc sander to sand the fingers flush with the box sides. Use the disc sander in the table saw to taper the top panel and top edges. On my box, I did this with a 10° angle setting on the saw, moving the fence a little at a time until I achieved the angled top surface I wanted (see photo 14).

Cut the lid from the bottom on the band saw. Align the cut so that the box separates right on the line between fingers. Before making the cut, check and adjust the band saw fence to allow for variations in the tracking of the band saw blade that could ruin all your hard work (see photo 15). Sand away the band saw marks with the belt and disc sander. Be careful to sand both side to side and front to back equally.

Use the 1/8" straight-cut bit in the router table to create the mortise for the lid tab to fit. Sliding the box lid between stops controls the position and length of cut (see photo 16). Use a 3/4" straight-cut bit to rout the mortises for the hinges. Set the height of cut to slightly less than half the closed thickness of the hinge. Use the fence to determine the location of the hinges on the box lid and base.

Holding the box lid and base together, sand all the outside surfaces of the box. Sand the edges very slightly with a sanding block. Apply the Danish oil finish, carefully rubbing between coats. When the oil has dried, install the hinges (see photos 17, 18).

Chapter 6

Wedding Ring Music Box

The first wedding ring music box that I made was for a man whose future bride had a dream about a small box with a music movement that played the Theme From Ice Castles. *This dream box was sized and lined to hold their wedding rings. He asked me to make it for her as his special wedding gift. It is a very special honor for a craftsman to be asked to help someone's dream come to life. I chose elm for this box and inlaid it with walnut, figured maple and pecan. The simple inlay technique uses shop-made oval templates and an inlay guide-bushing set that is readily available from most woodworking stores and catalogs.*

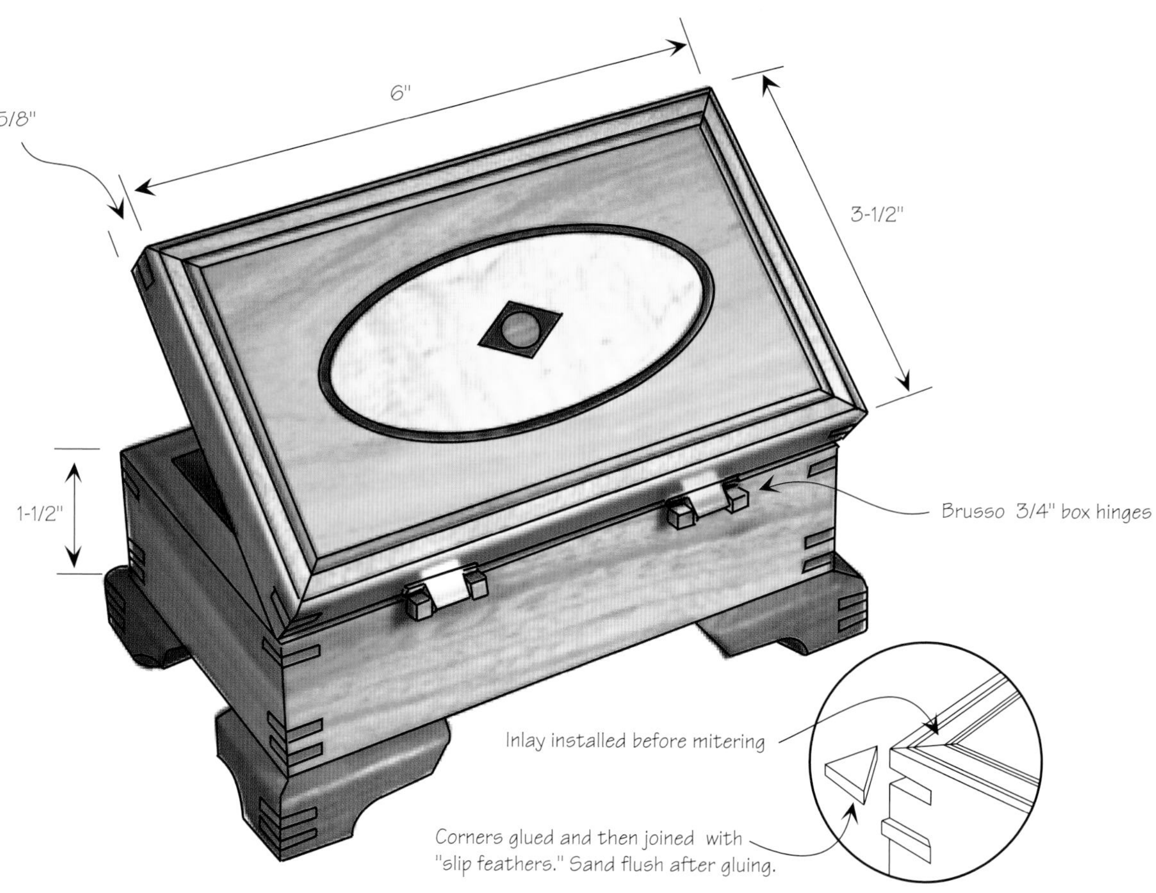

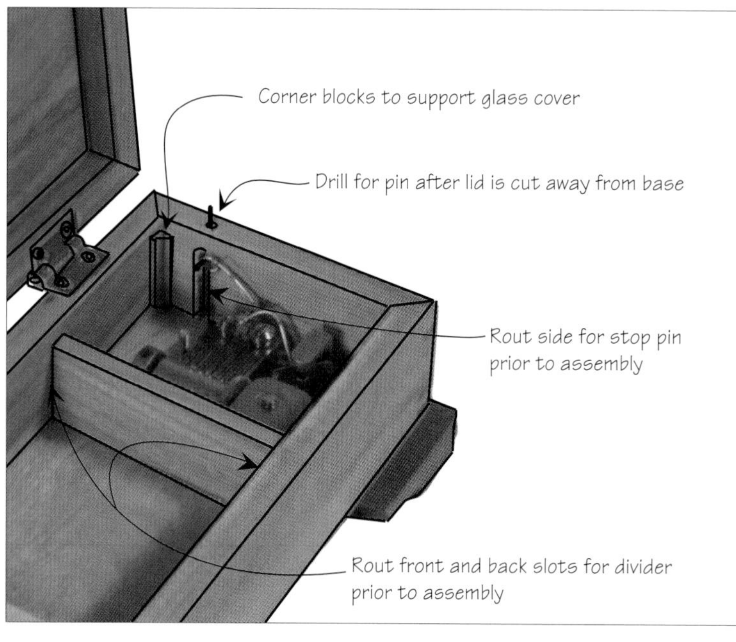

Make the Box

To make good use of material, resaw 4/4 elm stock, and plane it to a ⅜" thickness for the sides and top panel. Make the inlay banding using the same technique shown in making the Bracelet Box in chapter five. Rout the sides for the inlay to fit, glue the inlay in place (see photos 1 & 2). Cut the miters using the miter sled and stop block on the table saw (see photo 3).

Rout one end for the music box shutoff spring mechanism. Also rout the inside front and back of the box for the divider that will form the music box compartment (see photo 4).

Dado the ends, front and back for the top and bottom panels to fit. This can be done on the router table with a ⅛" bit or on the table saw with a ⅛"-kerfed blade.

Make the Inlay Templates

Draw an oval shape on paper (I used my computer's drawing program), and

1 Use a straight-cut bit in the router table to cut the channel for the inlay.

2 After gluing, clamp the inlaid parts together in pairs to hold the inlay tightly in position.

3 Cut the miters for the box parts using the miter sled on the table saw. Clamp a stop block in place to control the length of parts.

4 Rout the box end for the shutoff rod for the music movement. Next, using the same technique, rout the front and back for the interior divider to fit.

then stick the drawn shape onto the template stock with adhesive.

On the scroll saw, cut the oval shape into the original template. The scroll saw will leave some rough edges to even out and smooth with sandpaper. To finish the template, use a dowel with coarse sandpaper (see photo 5).

Clamp or screw this original template to another piece of plywood stock of the same dimensions. With a ⅛" bit, and using the inlay guide bushing with the brass bushing in place, rout a smaller version of the original template. This secondary template will be used to rout the space inside the walnut border to fit the figured maple within. To accurately position the stock for routing, nail strips to the back side of the templates. The space defined by the strips should be sized exactly to match the panel for the

Bill of Materials

PART NAME	NUMBER	DIMENSION TWL	COMMENTS
Ends	2	⅜ x 2¼ x 3½	
Front	2	⅜ x 2¼ x 6	
Back	2	⅜ x 2¼ x 6	
Interior Divider	1	3/16 x 1 x 3	
Top	1	⅜ x 3 x 5½	
Bottom	4	⅛ x 3 x 5½	Baltic birch plywood and template stock
Inlay Veneer	1	⅛ x 3 x 5½	Walnut
Inlay Veneer	1	⅛ x 1 x 1½	Walnut
Inlay Veneer	1	⅛ x 3 x 5½	Curly maple
Inlay Veneer	1	⅜-diameter plug	Cherry
Feet	4	⅝ x 11/16 x 4	
Slip Feathers			Cut from ⅛"-thick stock

Hardware

¾" Brusso Brass Box Hinges With Built-in Stops (1 pr.)
Music Movement (your choice of tune)

Making A Slip Feather Jig

I use a simple jig on the router table to cut the slots in the corners of boxes for "slip feathers" to fit. To make this jig, I first make a new low fence to fit the router table. Like all my router table fences, this one attaches at one end with a wing nut and at the other with a "c" clamp, allowing it to be easily and accurately adjusted.

Using hardwood blocks, build a saddle form to fit around the fence, leaving room on one side to allow for the thickness of the ¼" plywood used to form the base of the jig. There are no exact measurements required for making a working jig, but it may be helpful to size it to allow for the largest size boxes you will plan to make with "slip feathers".

Next, using the table saw, cut a hardwood block to form the cradle that holds the box for "slip feathering".

For making square boxes, the block should be cut using the saw arbor tilted to 45°. Use small screws or brads and glue to assemble the parts of the jig as shown in the drawing. I used screws on mine so that it could be taken apart and modified as necessary.

In using the jig, cut short sections of hardwood dowels to position the box for cutting the slip feathers. This keeps you from having to change the position of the fence for various cuts.

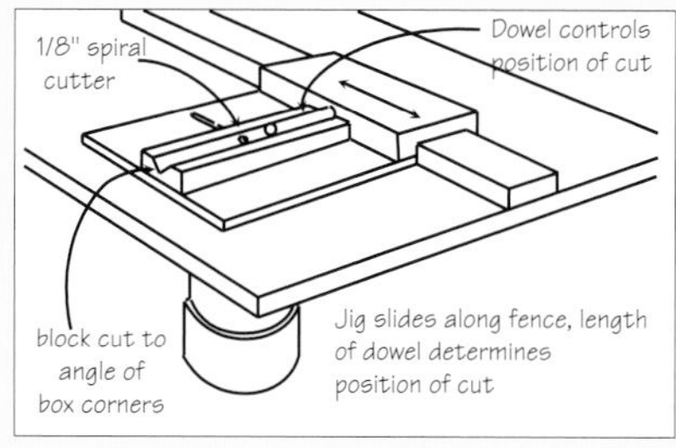

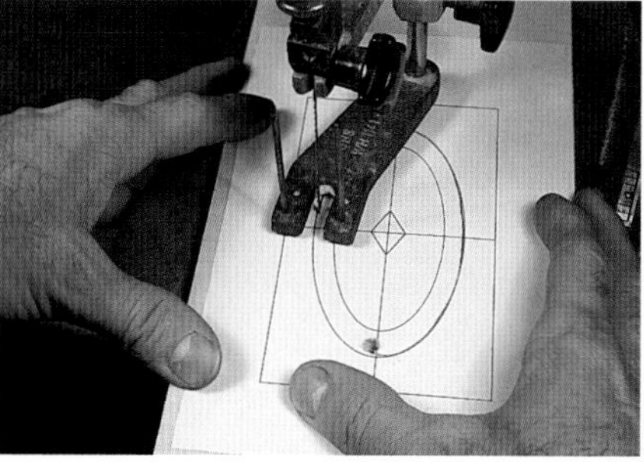

5 **Glue an oval shape to scrap plywood stock and, using a scroll saw, cut the oval shape into the primary template. The larger oval allows for the guide bushings, which will reduce the size of the final inlay piece.**

6 **Use the primary template to form the secondary template. I used screws to attach them to each other for routing.**

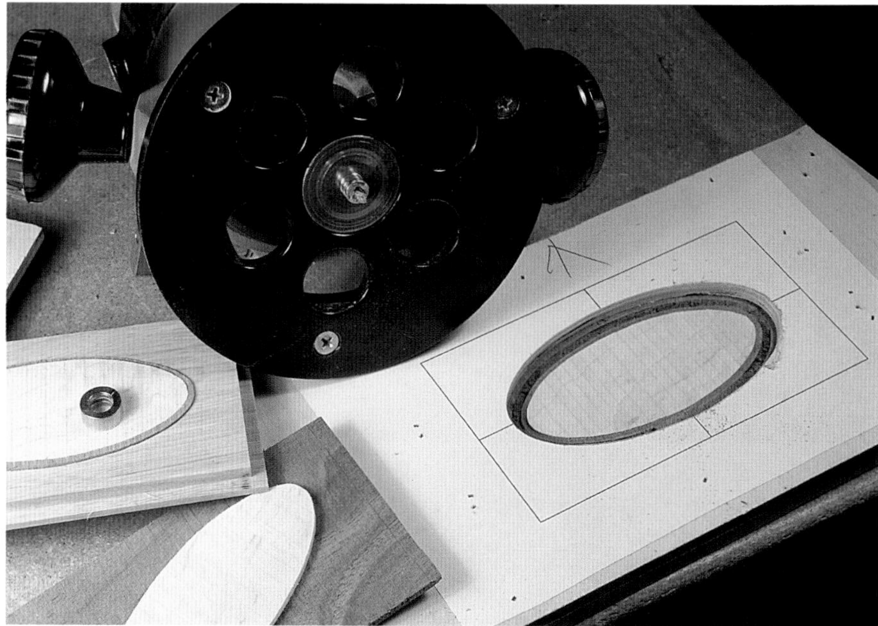

7 **Changing templates and guide bushings allows the various inlay parts to fit within each other. Use the brass bushing over the guide bushing to rout the inside shapes, then use the guide bushing without the brass bushing to cut the part to fit. Scrap stock brad nailed to the backs of the templates holds the workpieces in position for routing.**

top (see photos 6, 7 & 8).

Make a diamond template using the same techniques as used for making the oval templates. Cut the diamond shape with the scroll saw, then clean up the edges and finish the corners with a straight chisel (see photo 9).

In order to keep the inlay material from moving around while routing, the veneers must be taped to backing panels with double-stick carpet tape. The backing panels need to be cut to the same dimensions as the top panel to keep them from moving. Cut an extra panel at this time to serve as the box bottom.

Make and Install the Inlay

On the band saw, rip the inlay stock from solid wood. Before cutting, pass one side across the jointer to provide a good gluing surface. Leave the other side rough, to be finished when the box is sanded.

Insert the top panel into the space defined by the strips on the back of the original template. With the brass bushing in place, rout the stock away, forming the recess for the inlay to fit into. The depth of the cut should be just a bit less than the thickness of the veneers cut on the band saw.

Cut a piece of maple veneer slightly longer and wider than needed, and use carpet tape to attach the veneer to a backing piece. Insert the veneer with the backing piece into the smaller template. Rout the shape of the maple

8 Hold the guide bushing firmly to the side of the template as the bit is lowered into the stock. Hold the router firmly to the edge of the template as you follow around the oval shape.

9 Use a third template for routing the diamond shape that appears at the inside of the oval. Double-stick carpet tape holds the veneers in place as the small pieces are cut from the surrounding stock.

10 Use a ⅜" bit in the drill press to form the space for the center circle to fit. Use a ⅜" plug cutter to form the round inlay piece.

11 Use the ¾" straight-cut bit in the router table to form the shape of the box feet. I cut away most of the waste with the band saw before routing.

inlay using the guide bushing without the brass bushing in place.

Using the same template, insert a backing piece with walnut veneer taped in place. Then, using the guide bushing with the brass bushing in place, rout the inside shape into the walnut for the maple to fit.

Remove the walnut center piece, and replace it with the maple one. The walnut banding is very fragile; it will help give strength if the maple piece is glued in place before the next cut.

Change to the larger template, and insert the walnut-and-maple piece, with backing, into the space formed by the strips on the underside. Remove the brass bushing, and rout the walnut piece to fit into the top of the panel. Now, with the top panel in place and the brass bushing on the guide bushing, rout the channel around the edges of the top panel for the inlay pieces to fit. It may require a very light sanding on some edges for the inlay to fit the recess. Glue the inlay in place, with backing pieces to prevent marring the back of the panel with the clamps.

Rout the diamond shape inside the oval using the diamond template. After removing the brass bushing, use the same template with a backing piece to rout the veneer to fit the diamond. Fitting the veneer inside the diamond will require some handwork, either rounding the points of the diamond or using a chisel to finish the cut in the oval.

With a ⅜" bit, drill for the cherry plug to fit inside the diamond (see photo 10). After the plug is glued in place, the top panel can be sanded on the belt and disc sander.

Shape the Feet

To make the feet for the music box, stock must be milled to shape prior to assembly. This requires a ¾" straight-cut bit on the router table. Use stops to control the movement of the parts. To define the shape of the feet, gradually move the fence in small increments. Making a relief cut on the band saw can speed up the operation, reducing the number of router setups. You will find that if you make all the cuts from the right to the left, moving along the fence and reversing the stock at the middle of the cut, dangerous tear-out at the end of the cut can be avoided (see photo 11).

12 Assemble the box parts around the top, bottom and divider. Spread glue on the mitered surfaces, assemble, and then clamp the box securely.

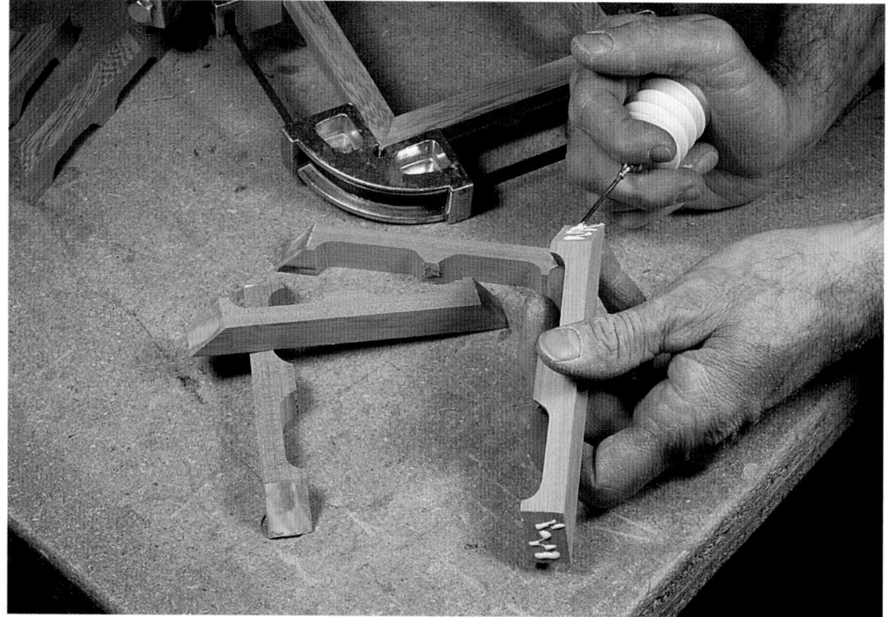

13 Spread glue on the miters, and clamp the box feet parts together until the glue dries.

14 Use the slip-feather guide on the router table to cut for the corner wedges to fit. Use stop pieces of varying lengths to control the positions of the slip feathers.

15 Use the same technique to slip-feather the corners of the feet.

Prepare for Assembly

Prior to assembly, make the interior divider. Square the routed slots in the box front and back square with a small chisel. Sand the interior surfaces of the box sides, top panel, divider and bottom.

Assemble the Box

Put glue on the mitered surfaces, and assemble the box around the top and bottom panels and the interior divider. The section that will be cut apart to form the feet can also be glued up now. Clamp the pieces together. On a small box like this, you can use rubber bands or band clamps (see photos 12, 13).

Using the slip-feather-cutting jig on the router table, cut recesses for splines to fit in the corners of the box and the feet (see photos 14, 15). Another view of this is shown in chapter thirteen, photo 4.

Cut walnut splines, and glue them in place in both the box and the feet. After the glue has set, use the belt and disc sander to bring the splines flush with the surrounding surface (see photo 16). After the splines have been sanded flush, use the band saw to cut the top of the box away from the base. Use the belt and disc sander to smooth the band saw cuts (see photo 17).

Rout a ⅛" mortise in the front of the lid for the lift tab.

Finish and Attach the Feet

Use the table saw to cut the individual feet apart from the assembled group. Set the miter slide at a 45° angle and the saw arbor at 90°. This operation can also be performed using the table saw fence with the saw arbor tilted, but

16 Spread glue into the slots, then press the slip feathers in place.

there is some risk of kickback.

Shape the edges of the feet with the ⅛" roundover bit in the router table (see photo 18). Then sand them with a dowel wrapped in sandpaper (see photo 19). Spread a bit of glue where the feet will contact the box, and carefully position the feet in place (see photo 20). After the glue has dried, drill for ⅛" dowels to connect the feet to the body of the box. After trimming the dowels flush with the surrounding material, use a sandpaper-wrapped dowel to finish the job.

As a final step in the attachment of the feet, use a fine rasp and then a sanding block to gently shape the areas between the feet.

Make the Pull

To form the outside profile, shape a strip of walnut using a ⅛" roundover bit. Use a 5⁄16" straight-cut router bit to form the tenon.

Cut the walnut strip into short pieces. Then, holding them together on edge, use the ⅛" roundover bit in the router table to shape the ends of the pulls. Holding the walnut pulls together as a block allows them to follow the fence and keeps them from tipping as they are routed. I always make extra pulls to use for other projects (see photos 21 & 22).

Use the sled on the table saw to finish forming the shoulders on the tenons. Then cut them apart, being sure that the tenon length matches the depth of the mortise cut in the box lid.

17 Use the band saw to cut the top of the box from the bottom. This cut must be planned carefully to allow for the interior divider and the music stop pin.

18 After cutting the assembled units apart and using a roundover bit in the router table to give them shape, hand sand the feet. Here I'm using the orbital sander as a sanding pad—with the power turned off.

19 Sand the inside contours of the feet with a dowel wrapped in sandpaper.

20 **Use ⅛" dowels to attach the feet. Glue the feet in place first, then after the glue has dried, use the drill press to drill for the dowels to fit. After trimming the dowels flush with the surrounding material, use a sandpaper-wrapped dowel to finish the job.**

21 **Shape the lid tabs on the router table. The center part is routed to fit the ⅛" mortise cut into the box lid. Use a ⅛" roundover bit to shape the tabs before they are cut to length.**

22 **Hold a set of tabs together for routing the ends. It's OK to make more than you need.**

23 **After the box is sanded and oil finished, rout for the hinges to fit. Clamp stop blocks to the router table to control the length of the cut, then change the location of the stop blocks to rout the opposite sides.**

Install the Hinges

Sand and finish the box with Danish oil. To mortise for the hinges to fit, use a ¼" straight-cut bit in the router table. Use the fence and stop blocks to position the box parts over the cutter for routing the hinge mortises. You will need to adjust the position of the stop blocks for cutting the opposite sides. Rout a test piece to check the accuracy of the setup. Square the corners of the hinge mortises with a straight chisel (see photo 23). Drill for the hinge screws with a Vix bit (see photo 24).

Install the Music Box Movement

Mark the locations of the holes for the music box movement with an awl onto a paper template.

Drill the required holes, using a block of wood underneath to keep the plywood bottom from splintering around the holes. Use the screws provided with the movement to attach it to the box. On the drill press, position the fence and stop blocks to drill for the music box stop pin. It may take some trial and error to bend the wire for the music box shut-off mechanism (see photos 25 & 26).

24 **Use a Vix bit in the electric drill to drill for the screws to fit the hinges.**

25 **Make a paper template for installing the music movement (I use business card stock.) Mark the locations of the holes with an awl.**

26 **I use a small brad as the bit when drilling for the stop pin on the drill press. When drilling the holes to attach the movement, use a wood block under the box to prevent splitting out the underside of the plywood bottom.**

Cutting Miters

Cutting accurate miters can be a challenge. Getting the angle just right is often a trial-and-error process and can get frustrating. I use two different sleds, or sliding tables, on the table saw to assist in cutting miters. The first is designed to use the table saw with the angle at 90°. This is used for narrow stock or stock that must be cut standing vertical on the table saw (Figure 1). To make this sled, I use a carpenter's square to set up the angled parts. This ensures that each side will be "perfect" in relation to the other. Even if one side were off one-half of a degree or more, the other would compensate, giving a tight-fitting miter.

To make this sled, first mill hardwood runners to the size of the miter guide slots on the top of the table saw. Check their fit. They should slide freely but have no side-to-side play. Use screws to attach one runner to a piece of 3/4" plywood, making sure the runner is square to the front edge of the plywood. Place the other runner in the miter guide slot on the table saw and, using screws, attach the plywood to it. Use a 45° tri-square to help position the first 45° strip to the sled. Use screws to hold it in place. Raise the blade of the table saw. Sliding the sled on the tabletop, cut into the sled, cutting the angled strip to length. Use a carpenter's square to position the matching angle fence on the opposite side, and attach it to the plywood with screws.

The second sled (Figure 2) uses the saw arbor tilted to 45°. This sled works best for wide stock. To make it, begin making the first sled. But when the runners are in place, turn the sled over. Using a 3/4" dado set in the table saw, make a cut in the sled top at 90° to the runners. The dado is for the fence to fit into. Plane the fence material down to 3/4", and hold it in place with screws from the underside.

You'll find the first sled is easy to use because it requires the table saw blade at the normal 90° setting. Stop blocks can be clamped in place to accurately cut pieces to length. The second sled requires the saw arbor to be tilted to 45°. I use a tri-square to check the angle, and I always make the first cut on scrap stock. These two sleds will make your mitering on the table saw easy and accurate.

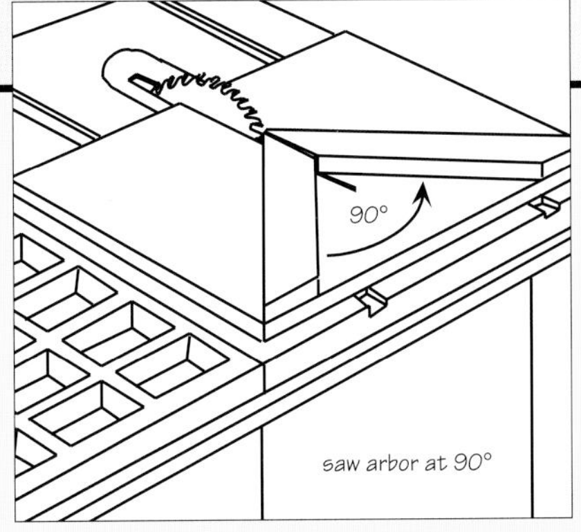

Figure 1

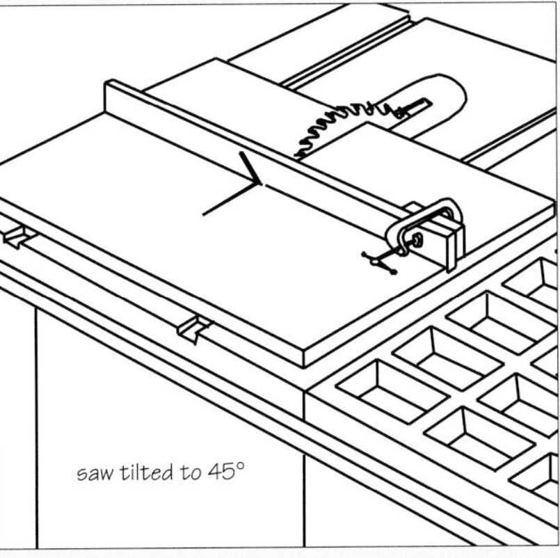

Figure 2

Chapter 7

Winter Woods Box

When I was a child in Memphis, Tennessee, I often went on family outings to Shelby Forest, a nature reserve on the Mississippi River. Walking in the woods there in the park is one of my earliest memories and continues to be a source of inspiration in my work. These days, I live in a small clearing in the forest just north of Eureka Springs, Arkansas. Our home sits on a narrow shelf, with a steep mountain to the north and a deep "holler" to the south. Walking in our woods has now become one of my daughter's earliest memories as well. This box is my attempt to share the tactile experience of a walk in the woods in winter.

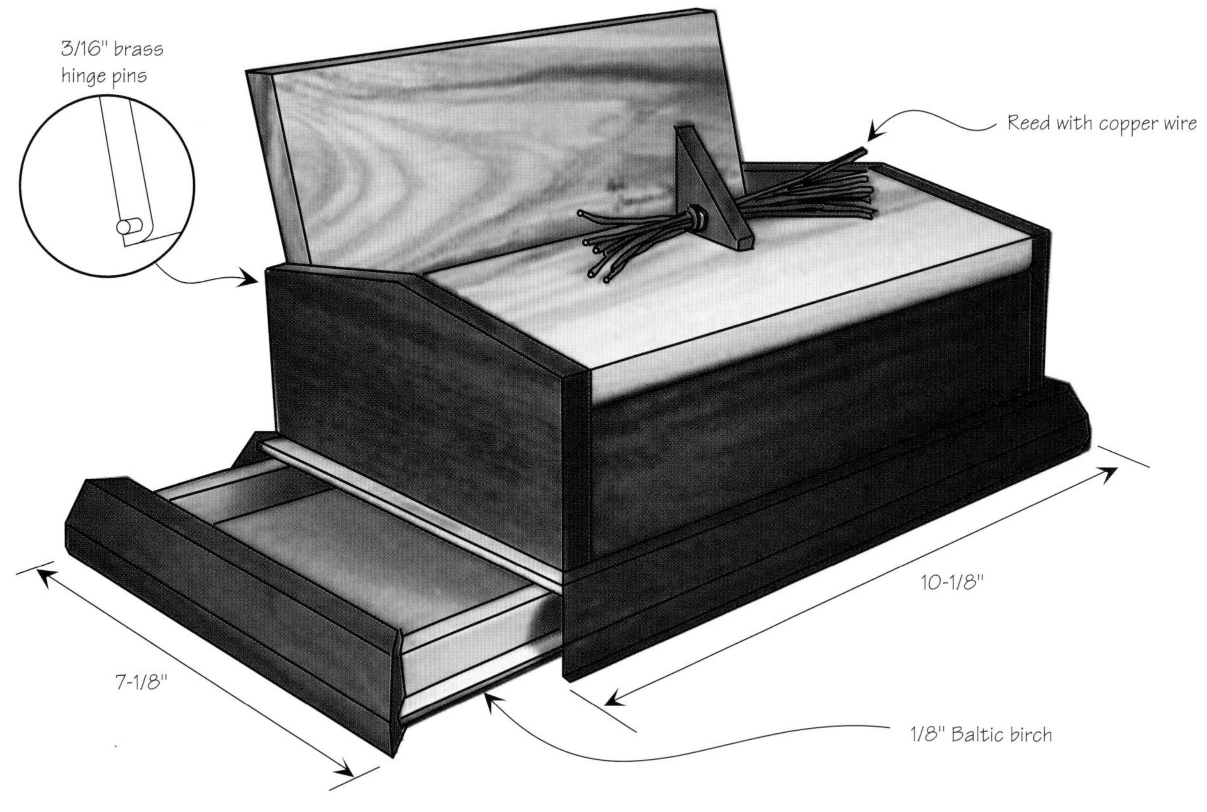

Bill of Materials

PART NAME	NUMBER	DIMENSION TWL	COMMENTS
Ends	2	3/8 x 2 7/8 x 6 1/16	
Front	1	3/8 x 1 3/4 x 8 5/8	Includes 3/16" tenons
Back	2	3/8 x 1 3/4 x 8 5/8	Includes 3/16" tenons
Lids	2	5/16 x 3 1/8 x 8 1/4	Resawn from contrasting 5/4 stock
Base Sides	2	5/8 x 1 1/8 x 10 1/8	
Base Ends	2	5/8 x 1 1/8 x 7 1/8	
Box Bottom	1	1/8 x 6 5/16 x 9 5/16	Baltic birch plywood
Drawer Sides	2	3/8 x 9/16 x 8 3/4	
Drawer Back	1	3/8 x 9/16 x 5 3/4	
Drawer Bottom	1	1/8 x 6 5/16 x 9 5/16	Baltic birch plywood
Hardware			
Hinge Pins	4	3/16 dia. x 3/4	Cut from 3/16" brass rod
Lid Stops	4	1/8 dowel x 1/2	Cut from 1/8" dowel
Pulls	2	5/16 x 1 1/2 x 3 1/4	Cut from stock
Reeds	18		For the pulls
Copper Wire	2	4"	12-gauge

Choosing the Wood

I often have small pieces of various hardwoods left over from my custom work. Many are highly figured but available in very limited quantities, enough for a box top but not for sides as well. The richness of black walnut makes the perfect frame for lesser-known American hardwoods. In this box, I used spalted pecan that has been resawn and bookmatched. The reed, an almost fragile material, invites a gentle touch. The Winter Woods Box also has a secret drawer hidden in its base.

Prepare the Stock

To make the best use of your materials, cut the stock to width before resawing and planing. Using the band saw and fence, resaw the walnut stock into pieces of equal thickness. Plane these to ⅜" thick. Then, joint one edge of the stock, and rip on the table saw to the required dimensions. I usually rip the stock to 1⁄32" oversize and then bring it to final size by passing it on edge through the planer. Another option is to joint the opposite side, so you won't have saw marks to sand away. Next, resaw the material for making the lids. Plane these to 5⁄16" thick, and joint one side.

Make the Box Body

With the cutoff sled or sliding table on the table saw, cut the box-body parts to size. Don't cut the lids to size yet. It is best to wait and get your final dimension from the trial-assembled box body.

To rout the mortises in the box ends, use a ⅛" bit in the router table. Set the height of the cutter 3⁄16" above the height of the table so that the mortises will be 3⁄16" deep. Check the depth with the dial gauge. To allow for glue and variations, I usually cut about 1⁄128" deeper than required. The fence should be set to allow for some waste to be sanded away after assembly.

Use a 1" straight-cut bit in the router table to cut the tenons on the front and back pieces (photo 1). Before cutting the tenons, I often make a relief cut on the table saw. This helps keep the wood from being grabbed and pulled into the router and scaring the daylights out of me, as it eases the cut. This precaution is required when making a large cut or when working with very hard wood like figured walnut.

1 Use a straight-cut bit in the router table to form the tenons on the box fronts and backs. Note the relief cuts made on the table saw to ease the router's job and to prevent it from pulling the workpiece into the cut. This is particularly needed when making a large cut or when working with hard wood like this figured walnut.

2 After the tenons are cut to fit the mortises, carefully measure and mark the locations for the hinge pins to fit the box ends.

Make a test piece before cutting your stock. Test the fit in the actual mortise. If the tenon enters easily, but does not fall out when you hold it up, you have a good fit.

3 Align the points marked for drilling on the drill press, adjusting the fence and then clamping stop blocks in place to position the holes accurately.

4 After positioning one stop block, drill through a piece of scrap wood and use it as an index piece to set up the opposite stop block so the hinge pins on opposite ends will be in perfect alignment. Note the box end on the lower right has already been drilled while the opposite stop block location is being determined.

5 With an ⅛" bit in the drill press, set up stop blocks and drill for the lid stop pins to fit.

6 Using an old carbide blade, cut the hinge pins to length on the table saw. I use $^3/_{16}$" brass welding rod. Gently round the ends of the hinge pins on the belt sander to make assembly easier.

To trim the tenons to width, use the table saw with the sled to cut away corners at the bottom of the fronts and backs. Align the first cut with the tenon shoulder. Then for the second cut, turn the piece on end, and readjust the stop on the fence. This will cut away a small corner, allowing the tenon to fit the width of the mortise.

Fit the Lids

Assemble the box ends, fronts and backs with the tenons in the mortises. Measure the exact length of the opening. Using the sled on the table saw, cut the lids to fit the opening. I generally cut the lids to exactly the length measured and then make a second cut after bumping the stop over just slightly. This gives clearance for the lid to open and close without scraping the sides.

To mark for the hinge pin holes, use a straightedge along the top front edge of the trial-assembled box to mark the location of the box lid, and then mark in ¼" for the position of the pin. Measure up from the edge of the box front ¼" plus $^1/_{16}$" for clearance for opening and closing (photo 2). These measurements will give the center points for the holes on the box ends. I also mark out the edges of the holes so that it is easier for me to see that I have accurately set up the drill press with the brad-point bit.

Use a drill press to drill the hinge-pin holes in the end pieces. I use a $^3/_{16}$" drill bit that I broke off shorter and reground to a brad point in order to eliminate flex. Use stop blocks and a fence to control the position of the holes. To make sure that the holes on opposite sides are aligned, I drill an index piece

7 Before the box lids are cut to length, mark the matching resawn panels so the face and back sides will not get confused.

8 Use a trial-assembled box to check the fit as the lids are cut to length. I use a crosscut sled on the table saw and use a stop block to make certain the matching lids are the same length and fit to close tolerances.

9 When drilling for the hinge pins to fit, an accessory clamped to the table of the drill press helps hold the lid while a stop block positions it.

10 After drilling one end of the lid, reposition the stop block for drilling the hinge hole in the opposite end. Note the structure holding the face of the jig square to the base.

which will help to reset the stop (photos 3, 4).

With a ⅛" bit in the drill press, mark and drill for the lid stops. Use the drill press fence and stop blocks to control the position (photo 5).

Use 3⁄16" brass welding rod for the hinge pins. With an old carbide blade in the table saw and using a cutoff sled and stop block, cut the hinge pins to length (photo 6). Slightly smooth the ends of the pins by rolling them against the 6" x 48" belt sander. This will make the box easier to assemble.

Drill for the hinge pins to fit the lids (photos 7, 8). To hold the lids vertical for drilling, make a fixture to fit a standard drill press (photo 9). My Shopsmith works as a horizontal borer, but this fixture is just as easy and accurate to use, and it works on a standard drill press. I always start with a test piece and check the position of the hole carefully with a dial caliper. Adjust the position of the stop to drill the opposite side (photo 10).

11 After putting one hinge pin in a lid and fitting it to a box end, use a sliding T bevel to transfer the angle to the table saw for cutting the correct angle where the lids meet.

12 Note the pencil mark at the center of the box end to indicate the width of the cut on the table saw when cutting the lids to width. I use a trial-and-error system to get a good fit, making my first cut wide and then narrowing the distance from the blade to the fence.

13 Rout for the lid pulls prior to assembly. Stop blocks clamped to the router table control the length of the cut, while the fence is set to position the mortises equidistant from the ends of the lids.

14 Assemble the box with glue, and clamp as needed.

Now, the lids can be cut to their final width. Slip the ⅛" birch stop pins in place in the box ends. Then, with the hinge pins in place, fit a lid to an end piece (see photo 11). Mark the center line where the two lids will meet, and mark the box lid at that same point. Then with a sliding "T" bevel, transfer the angle formed by the lid and box end to the table saw (see photo 12). Use the mark on the lid to help set the fence to cut the lids to the required size. After cutting the opposite lid to the same size, check the fit where the two lids meet. If they are too tight and do not allow a bit of space for expansion of the material, adjust the table saw fence just a bit narrower, and cut the lids again.

Assemble the Box

Before assembly, rout mortises in the lids for the pulls to fit. Use a ⅛" straight-cut bit in the router table. Adjust the fence so that the cutter will be at the center of the width of the lids. Control the length of cut with stop blocks (see photo 13).

Use a glue syringe to put glue into the mortises. With the hinge pins installed, fit the front and back tenoned parts into one end. Then carefully align the parts and slip the other end in place. If they fit tightly, no clamping will be necessary. Open and close the lids to make sure that the box is square (see photo 14).

Use the table saw to trim the box ends to conform to the shape of the lids (see photo 15). Duct tape will hold

15 Use the table saw, or the band saw tilted at an angle, to cut the box ends to shape. Taping the lids closed with duct tape keeps them from coming in contact with the saw blade. Plan your cut to allow for some stock to be sanded flush on the stationary belt sander.

16 Use the mitered cutoff sled to cut the base parts to length. Note the C-clamp holding a stop block in place to control the length of the parts.

17 After the base parts are cut to length, use the table saw with a 1/8" kerf blade to cut the dadoes for the box bottom and drawer to fit.

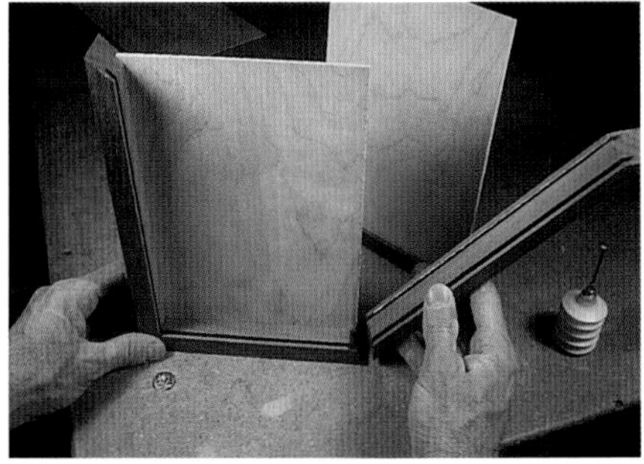

18 Use glue in the dadoes as the base is assembled around the box bottom and drawer. Glue the drawer bottom to the drawer front but not the sides. Glue the box bottom to all the rest of the parts, but not the drawer front. Do not glue the miters intersecting the drawer front. This will allow the two parts to slide apart to open.

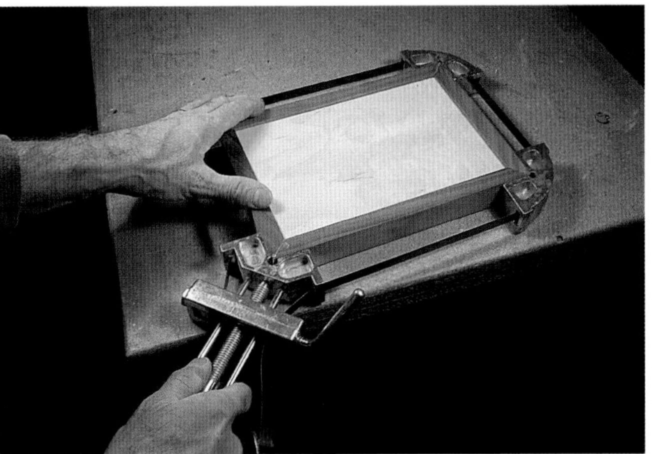

19 Use a band clamp to hold the parts together as the glue sets.

20 Use the table saw, with the arbor tilted to 15°, to cut the base to shape. Be careful to check which side is up before cutting. The base should be upside down on the table saw to be shaped properly.

the lids closed during the cut. Then using the 6" × 48" belt sander, sand the ends level to the lids and sand the ends flush with the front and back.

Make the Base

Plane walnut stock to size for the base. Then cut the pieces to length using the mitered sled on the table saw. Use a stop block to control the length of the pieces, changing the location of the stop block for the two different lengths (photo 16).

Use a 1/8" kerfed saw blade to cut the channels for the plywood to fit. These cuts should be 1/8" from each edge (photo 17).

Cut 1/8" Baltic birch plywood for the box and drawer bottoms. These should be sized to exactly fit the space allowed less about 1/64" each dimension to allow for sliding.

To assemble the base, first sand the birch plywood pieces, gently rounding the edges with sandpaper. Then glue three edges of the top piece, and only one edge of the bottom piece, to fit in the base dadoes. Put glue in the dadoes, and also the corners, before assembling and clamping. Be careful not to glue the piece that will become the drawer front except where it fits to the drawer bottom. Clamp the pieces together (photos 18, 19).

Trim the base to shape on the table saw with the arbor tilted to 22½°. The base must be upside down when cutting. First cut the sides and then the ends (photo 20).

Use hardwood stock to form the drawer sides and back. Rout the top edges with a 1/16" roundover bit in the router table. Then use the 45° cutoff sled to cut the angles and the straight 90° cutoff sled where the drawer sides meet the front. I use a jig to hold the parts in position for gluing and nailing in place with brads.

21 **Use the 1" straight-cut bit in the router table to shape the tenons on the ends of the lid pulls. Set the height of cut to just under the depth of the mortises in the lids. Check the fit of the tenon to the box lid. Rather than using test pieces in this operation, I just plan to make more than are necessary and adjust the fence or router height as needed.**

22 **Drilling the holes in the lid pulls can be done either before or after shaping the tenons. I use a 1/4" brad-point bit in the drill press and position the hole slightly off center.**

23 **Cut the tenons to the proper width on the table saw. Use the sled and a stop block clamped to the fence to position the cut.**

24 **The final shaping of the pull is done using an angled sled on the table saw. This sled, with no permanent fence, allows temporary fences to be tacked in place. The angled sled also allows for the use of clamps to hold workpieces securely.**

Make the Pulls

Cut and plane stock to 5/16" thick, and then cut it to width and length as specified for the pulls. As in making the tenons for the box front and back, use the 1" straight-cut bit in the router table to form tenons on the ends (see photo 21). This can be done either before or after the holes are drilled into which the reeds will fit (see photo 22). Use the cutoff sled on the table saw to trim the tenons to length. Next, using another cutoff sled as shown in the picture, set up an angled fence and stops to cut the pulls to shape (see photos 23 & 24).

Fit the Box to the Base

Use a straight-cut bit in the router table to trim the box to fit the base. Set the height of the bit to 1/8" so that it will fit down into the base. I always make my first cut on a test piece so I can check the fit before routing on the assembled box. Trim each side to fit, then check the fit with the base. Adjust the fence as needed to get a good fit.

Use the orbital sander to sand the box parts. Lightly sand the edges with a sanding block to smooth. Hand sand the pulls with sheets of sandpaper.

Apply three coats of Danish oil finish. I apply one heavy coat of oil, and wait about half an hour before applying the second. After the second coat starts to get a bit sticky, I rub it out with a dry cloth. Wait about 24 hours before applying the third coat and, like the second coat, rub it out when it just starts to get sticky.

Use clear all-purpose glue to attach the box to its base. I use masking tape to hold the parts together as the glue dries (photo 25).

Cut eight or nine pieces of reed to fit through the 1/4" hole in each pull. Dye the reed with dark brown Rit fabric dye before cutting it to length. Push a 4" piece of 12-gauge copper wire through the hole after the reeds are in place. Carefully wrap the wire tightly around the reeds on both sides of the hole, first one side and then the other, reversing directions of twist on the two sides (photo 26). Use carpenter's glue applied in the mortise to hold the pull itself in place. Use flocking material or Ultrasuede as a lining as a lining for the base drawer and the inside of the box.

25 Use clear glue to attach the box to the base. Then use masking tape to clamp the parts together as the glue dries.

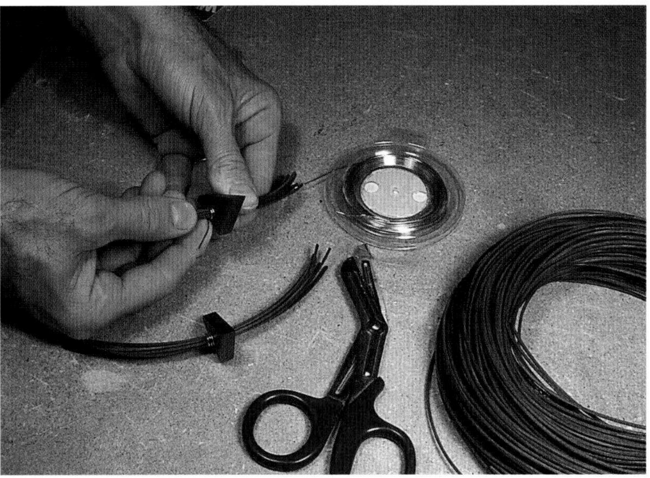

26 Use copper wire twisted tightly around the reeds to hold them in place before gluing the pulls into the box lids.

My Router Table

My "router tables" are quick and easy—just a router turned upside down, bolted to a piece of ¾" plywood and clamped to the workbench. When I'm done with it, I can unclamp it and put it away, saving precious floor space in my crowded shop. I use a "pivot" fence with my router tables, which gives a great deal of accuracy, and is so easily made that I can make them in different configurations as I need them (see Figure 1). The pivot fence is simply a piece of wood with a hole through it for a bolt. The bolt attaches it to the router table, and the other end is secured by a C-clamp.

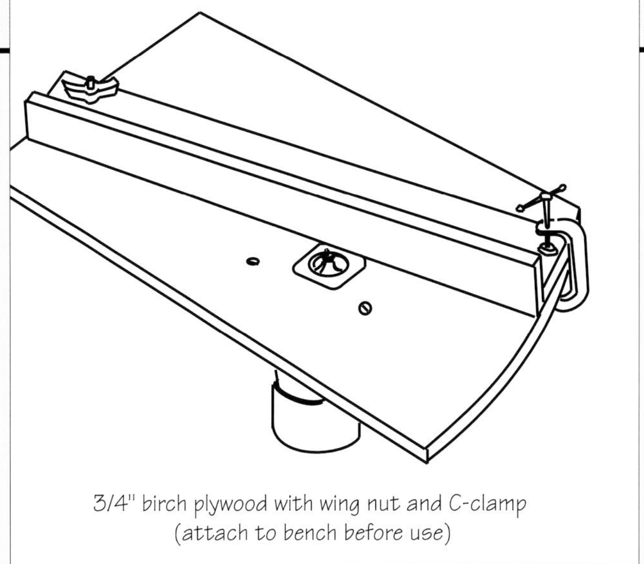

3/4" birch plywood with wing nut and C-clamp (attach to bench before use)

Figure 1

Make the Inserts

To safely accommodate various router bits, inserts will have to be made to fit the hole in your router table through which the bit emerges. I usually get around to making the inserts sometime after the table has been in use for a while.

First, cut several square inserts on the table saw to the exact same size. Round the corners to a ¼" radius by standing them together on the router table with a ¼"-radius ball-bearing roundover bit. You can use ¼" maple, plastic, birch plywood or Lucite. Use a fence to cover most of the cutter and to help guide the pieces squarely into the cutter—never do an operation like this with a router held freehand.

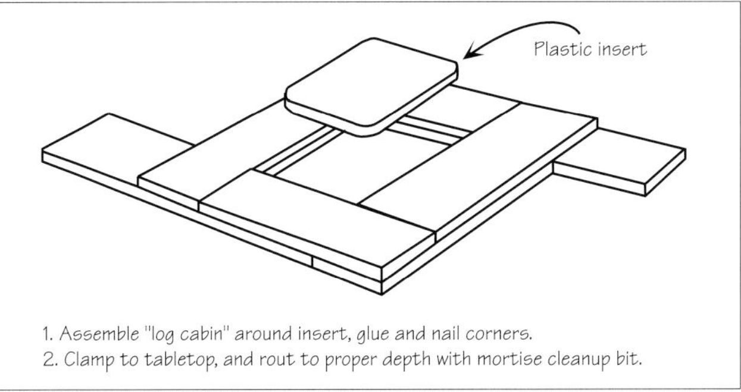

1. Assemble "log cabin" around insert, glue and nail corners.
2. Clamp to tabletop, and rout to proper depth with mortise cleanup bit.

Figure 2

Make the Template

With eight strips of ¼" plywood, construct a template around the inserts. Overlap the plywood at the corners. This will build a template the exact same size as the inserts (see Figure 2). Glue and nail the pieces to each other while surrounding the inserts.

If you want it to look neat, you can cut the plywood pieces to the exact length needed. Remember to make the template large enough so there is room for clamps on it as well as the router base.

Rout the Table for the Insert

Clamp the template in place on the table, and rout for the inserts to fit. I use a ½"-diameter mortise cleanup bit. Adjust the depth of cut so that the bit protrudes beneath the template equal to the thickness of the inserts. Provided the ¼"-radius cutter is precise, the inserts and recess routed for them should fit perfectly. If they are just a bit tight in the corners, sand them a bit or touch them up with a fine rasp.

Chapter 8

Men's Jewelry Box

In designing a box, I often imagine how it will be used, where it will be placed and where a person will stand when opening it. These considerations impact its usefulness and appearance. I designed this box to be slightly asymmetrical. With the back lid being thicker, it has a natural stopping point to prevent it from opening too far. No special or expensive hardware is needed. It uses the same hinge method and mortise-and-tenon joinery as the Winter Woods Box. The front lid, so as not to block access to the interior, needs to open to full width. The single pull offers a clear sequence in opening.

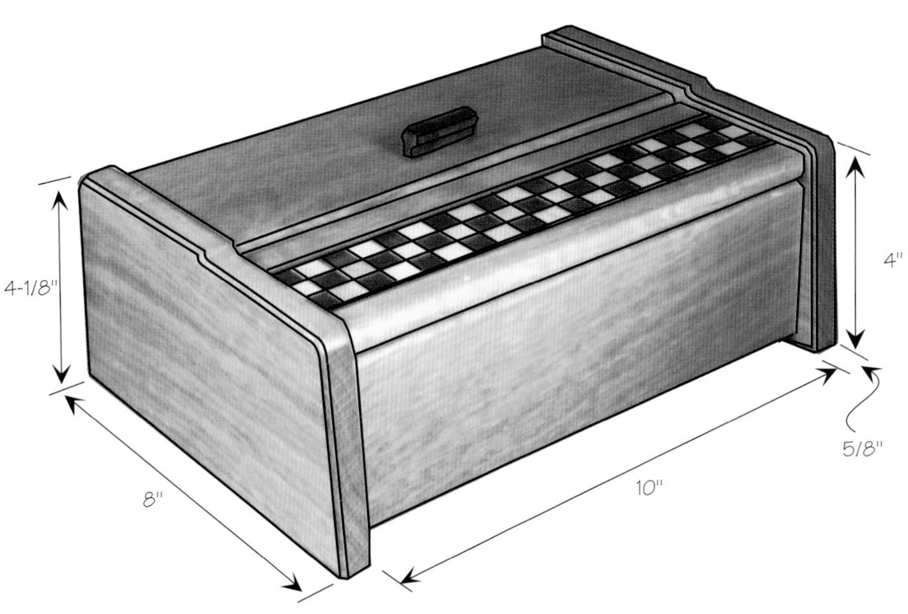

Bill of Materials

PART NAME	NUMBER	DIMENSION TWL	COMMENTS
Ends	2	5/8 x 4 1/8 x 8	
Front	2	1/2 x 3 x 10 1/2	Includes 1/4" tenons
Back	2	1/2 x 3 x 10 1/2	Includes 1/4" tenons
Lid	1	5/8 x 3 3/4 x 10	
Lid	1	1/2 x 3 1/4 x 10	
Bottom	1	1/8 x 6 1/4 x 10 1/4	Baltic birch plywood
Tray	1	1 1/16 x 3 x 9 9/16	
Tray Ends	2	3/16 x 1 1/8 x 3 1/16	
Tray Dividers	2	3/16 x 7/8 x 2 1/4	
Tray Supports	2	1/8 x 1/4 x 6	
Hardware			
Lid Stops	2	1/8 x 1/4 x 3/4	
Hinge Pins	4	3/4	Cut from 3/16 brass rod

Choosing the Lumber

I chose white oak for this box because I had some in my shop that was just the right thickness for planing down to make the parts. I have made similar boxes in maple and walnut. As with most of the boxes in this book, I suggest that you use the woods you have at hand, allowing your own lumber-hunting adventures to have as much an impact on your box making as my instructions.

Form the Box Ends

First, mortise the ends of the box. Use the router table and fence with a 3⁄16" straight-cut bit. Position the mortises with stop blocks, changing the locations of the blocks for mortising the opposite ends. (The Inlaid Walnut Ring Box shows this operation in detail.) To accurately position the opposite mortises, perform the same operation on thinner stock and use that as an index piece for routing the opposite mortise. To avoid breaking the fragile bits, I cut to the full depth of the mortises in two steps. Check the depth of the mortise with the dial caliper.

With a 1⁄8" straight-cut bit in the router table, rout the positions for the bottom panel, the tray slides and the lid rest. To keep the cuts from extending through the ends of the stock, use the router table for this job rather than the table saw. Please note that the positions of the lid rests are different on opposite ends, allowing clearance for the tray to be removed.

Make the Front and Back

To form the tenons, first make a relief cut. Use the sled on the table saw to perform this operation. The relief cut will ease the routing process by keeping the workpiece from being pulled into the cut. Use a stop block to accurately position the cut. Form the tenons themselves on the router table with a 1" straight-cut bit (see photo 1).

Cut the dadoes in the front and back for the bottom to fit. This can be done either on the router table, with a 1⁄8" straight-cut bit, or on the table saw, with a 1⁄8" kerfed blade.

1 Use the router table to route the tenons after the mortises are formed in the box ends. Note the relief cut made on the table saw to ease the router's work. This is crucial when making such a large cut. I have removed the safety blocking to give a better view.

With the table saw and sled, trim the tenons to width to fit the the mortises.

Make the Lids

To make the inlay for the front lid, cut blocks of wood to 1⁄2" × 3⁄4" × 13⁄4". Glue them together in an alternating pattern. Rip to form 1⁄2" × 3⁄4" × 13⁄4" square stock. Rearrange and reglue with edge banding. Rip thin strips for inlay.

For this box, I chose the easy way out and used an inlay design left over from other projects. If you want ideas for making your own inlay, you might want to start with patterns like that used for the Inlaid Walnut Ring Box. My first book, *Creating Beautiful Boxes With Inlay Techniques*, shows how to make the patterns used here. These patterns can be a starting point for your own personal experimentation in making inlay.

On the router table, rout the space for the inlay to fit. Set the height of cut just under the thickness of the inlay. For this, lay the inlay strip down on the table and check it against the position of the bit. Move the fence to widen the cut so that it nearly fits the inlay strip.

Joint one edge of the inlay strip. To size the inlay to fit the routed channel, adjust the fence position on the router table and raise the height of the straight-cut bit.

Spread glue in the routed channel, and press the inlay in place. Spread the clamping pressure and prevent marking the box lid by using clamping blocks.

Sand the inlay flush with the surrounding wood. This can be done with a belt sander, or on the 6" × 48" stationary belt sander. Check your progress regularly to avoid changing the thickness of the workpiece.

Trial-assemble the box to test the fit. Measure the opening, and cut the box lids to exact length. The sled and stop blocks on the table saw work well for making sure both lids are exactly equal in length. After cutting the lids to a perfect fit, adjust the stop on the sled a very slight amount to make the final

2 Use the router table to form the template that will be used to shape the ends of the box. A stop block clamped to the surface of the router table controls the length of the cut.

3 With the table saw sled, cut the angles in the edges of the template.

4 After all the mortises are cut, use the sled to cut the angles in the box ends.

5 Use a disc sander to round the top corners of the box end template to shape. I just penciled in the desired radius on the corners and then carefully sanded. A little bit at a time gives the best results.

cut, providing side clearance for opening and closing.

To provide clearance for opening, rout the outside edges of the box lids with a ¼" radius roundover bit in the router table.

Rout a small mortise for the pull on the back lid. Use the ⅛" straight-cut bit in the router table. This is similar to routing for the pulls in the Winter Woods Box except that the wood grain is oriented parallel to the fence.

Shape the Ends

The ends of the box are shaped to conform to the lids' change in thickness. To do this, and to give the box tops their round profile, make a template exactly the same size as the box ends. Use a scrap of ¾" plywood left over from another project.

Adjust the router table fence to ⅛", and with a straight-cut bit, rout the template between stops. Perform this same operation on the box ends, remembering to turn one end upside down so that the box ends will form a matched pair (see photo 2).

Set up either a miter gauge on the table saw, or a sled with the desired angle, and cut both the template and box ends to finished shape (see photos 3, 4). Then, on the band saw, cut a small radius on the top corners of the template. I used a radius of about ⅜", but this need not be exact. Finish the band sawn radius smooth with the disc sander (see photo 5).

Using the template, pencil the shapes of the radius on the box ends, and band saw away the excess on the outside of the line. One at a time, clamp the template over the ends, and rout the shapes to conform to the template. Use the template-following router bit (see photo 6).

Hinge the Lids

This technique is explained fully in the chapter on making the Winter Woods Box. Carefully lay out the position of the hinge pin on the box end, and then, with the drill bit in position to drill the hinge hole, adjust the fence and stop blocks on the drill press. Remember to drill the same hinge holes in the template so that you will have a record of the setup for future boxes. You will need to change the setup of the stop blocks for drilling opposite ends.

Drill the hinge-pin holes in the lids, again using the same setup as shown for the Winter Woods Box. The stop block will have to be adjusted for drilling the holes for the opposite ends of each lid. Then cut a 3/16" brass welding rod to length for the hinge pins. Measure the holes in both the box end and lid with a dial caliper. Add them up to get the length of the pins required.

Assemble the Box

Rout all the edges of the box ends, front, back and lids with a 45° chamfering bit. Then sand all the parts, progressing from coarse to extra fine. Start out with 180-grit and finish with 320-grit. Use a sanding block on the lid ends to prevent rounding them over. Put the hinge pins in place in the lids.

Put glue in the mortises and on the surface of the box ends where the front and back parts will contact. Place the tenons on the front and back pieces into the mortises of one end, fit the lids in place, and then slip the other end in place. Getting these parts to align all at the same time can be a challenge. Using a couple of folded business cards as shims will help to position the lids at the right height as the box is pulled together. Check as the box is clamped together to make certain it is square and that the lids have proper clearance. (see photos 7, 8).

6 With the template and box end carefully aligned and firmly clamped to the workbench, shape the box ends, using a template-following router bit. I prefer to trace the shape on the workpiece and remove most of the waste with the band saw before routing.

7 This photo shows all the parts ready for assembly. Note the mortises, the tray-support pieces already glued in place, and the dadoes for the bottom panel to fit.

8 Assemble all the parts at one end, then apply glue to the mortises for the opposite end, and clamp the box together.

9 The tray is shaped by making a series of cuts and using an offset fence clamped to the top of the table saw. Raise the blade in small increments and turn the workpiece end for end as the cove is formed. You can alter the angle of the fence as you go to change the shape and width of cut.

10 Use a 3⁄16" straight-cut bit in the router table to cut the slots for the tray dividers to fit. Using stops clamped in place on the router table will control the length of cut.

11 A dowel wrapped in sandpaper will remove the saw marks left by cove cutting.

Make the Sliding Tray

The sliding tray for the interior of the box is made using the table saw and a fence clamped at an angle to form the cove. Determining the correct angle for the fence is a trial-and-error process. Raise the height gradually, changing the angle of the fence until you get the cove you want. In order to form a double cove cut with a very slight divider in the middle, I reversed the stock, taking two passes for each change of blade height (see photo 9).

Use a large dowel wrapped in sandpaper to clean up the cove cut. Change grits gradually from coarse to fine. To speed up this operation, a curved scraper can be used (see photo 10).

Put the 3⁄16" straight-cut bit in the router table, and raise the height enough to rout for the dividers in the trays. Slide the tray between stop blocks to rout for the dividers to fit (see photo 11).

Cut the divider parts to length, then use a 1⁄8" roundover bit to shape the ends to fit the routed spaces. Sand the dividers thoroughly before gluing them in place.

Cut the tray ends to length. Rout the inside edges, the top edges and the ends of the tray with a 1⁄16" roundover bit in the router table.

Sand the end pieces before gluing them in place. Glue the ends of the tray bodies to attach the end pieces, and clamp them in place. To strengthen the joint, drill 1⁄8" holes in the ends of the trays for dowels. You can also use a brad nailer to attach the ends.

After assembling the box, use a straight-cut bit in the router table to trim the ends of the tray to fit down over the tray support.

Make the Pull

The pull is made using the same tenoning techniques as used for the pulls on the Winter Woods Box. Form the tenon on the ends of the pull before it is cut apart.

Form the inner shape with a core-box bit; form the outside shape with a chamfering bit (see photos 12, 13). Use the sled on the table saw to finish shaping the tenons.

Hand sand the outside shape of the pull with sandpaper. Use a piece of sandpaper wrapped on a dowel for the inside cove shape.

Apply three coats of Danish oil, and rub with a dry cloth. Glue the pull in place.

12 **Making the pull for the Men's Jewelry Box starts with a cove cut on the router table.**

13 **Use a straight-cut router bit to cut the tenon on the end of the pull. After the tenon is formed, the pull can be cut from the walnut stock for further shaping.**

Chapter 9

Pin Cabinet

The sassafras and ebonized cherry Pin Cabinet evolved from earlier designs and incorporates techniques from the Half-Turned Box. I often play with the parts of projects while they are under way, using them to stimulate my imagination for developing new work. I find this more effective than sitting at the drawing board, struggling to come up with ideas. Most exciting of all, it allows me to expand my use of new techniques into new designs. The Pin Cabinet is made to hold pins, necklaces and hook-type earrings, using fabric wings and brass pins for hanging.

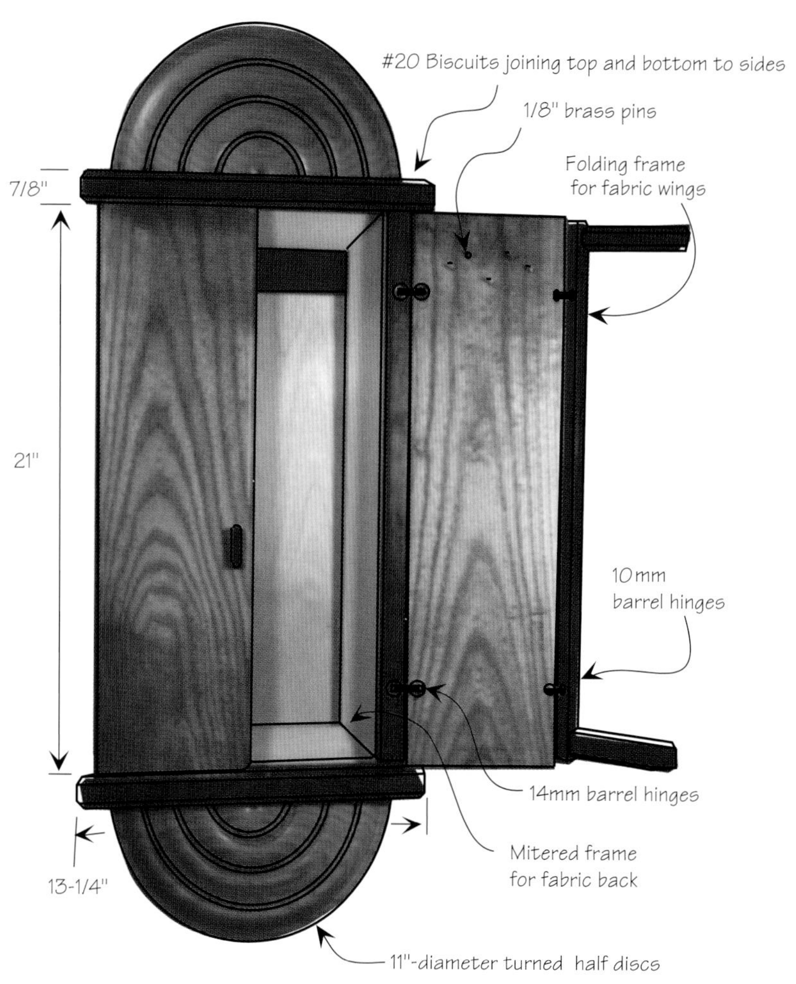

Bill of Materials

PART NAME	NUMBER	DIMENSION TWL	COMMENTS
Top	1	⅞ x 4⅛ x 13¼	
Bottom	1	⅞ x 4⅛ x 13¼	
Sides	2	¾ x 2¾ x 21	
Cross Stretcher	1	¾ x 3¼ x 10½	
Back Panel	1	¼ x 11 x 18¼	Baltic birch plywood
Doors	2	¾ x 6 x 20-16/16	
Hanger Parts	2	⅝ x ⅞ x 20½	Verticals
Hanger Parts	4	⅜ x ⅞ x 4¾	Horizontals (length includes ½" tenon)
Turnings	2	1 x 5½ x 11	
Interior Frame	2	⅝ x 1⅜ x 20⅞	Cut at angle
Interior Frame	2	⅝ x 1⅜ x 10⅜	
Hardware			
Biscuits	10	#20	
Barrel Hinges	2 pairs	14mm	
Barrel Hinges	2 pairs	10mm	
Necklace Hangers	10	⅛-thick x ¾-long	Cut from ⅛" brass rod
Brass Bullet Catches	2	5⁄16	

1 With the top and bottom pieces clamped to the workbench, cut the biscuit slots. Cut the slots for the sides first, then reposition the biscuit joiner fence for the top and bottom.

2 Carefully measure the opening between sides before cutting the cross stretcher.

3 Cut the angle on the cross stretcher after the dado is cut.

Make the Carcass

Cut the sides, top and bottom to dimension, then mark the locations for the biscuits. Cut the biscuit slots into the ends of the side pieces with the biscuit joiner. Then, adjust the fence of the biscuit joiner to cut the slots into the top and bottom (see photo 1).

Assemble the carcass for a trial fit with the biscuits in place. Then measure the exact distance for cutting the cross stretcher at the back of the cabinet. The cross stretcher performs several functions: It helps to square the cabinet during assembly; it gives the cabinet additional strength; and it provides a hanging point (see photo 2). Test fit the cross stretcher in the carcass, marking it, and the cabinet sides, for the biscuit slots. Cut biscuit slots for the cross stretcher, top and sides.

Cut a dado in the cross stretcher for the back panel to fit. Use a ¼" dado blade in the table saw for this operation.

Cut the 15° angle in the cross stretcher for the hanger to fit (see photo 3). Cut the same angle in the hanger strip.

4 Before routing the sides for the back panel to fit, rout a test piece. Check for alignment with the dado in the back stretcher.

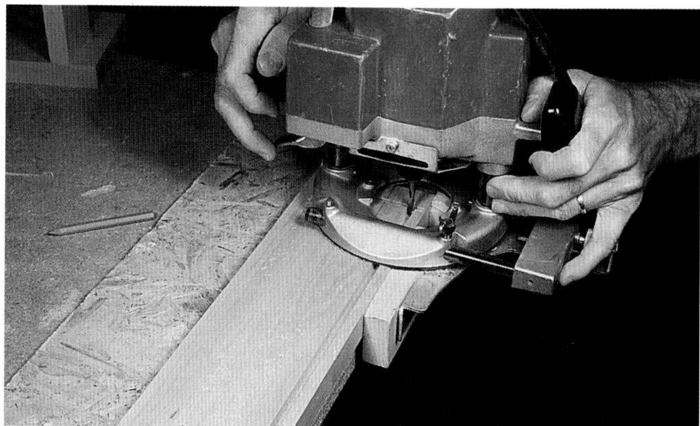

5 Rout the bottom and sides for the back to fit. Mark start and stop points on the workpiece to keep the dado from interfering with the biscuit slots.

6 Use the router table, fence and stops to rout the mortises in the internal hangers. Make the mortises in steps, raising the cutter in increments until you reach the required mortise depth.

7 Cut the shoulders on the tenons first. A stop block clamped to the fence on the sled positions the parts.

Use the plunge router, fence and ¼" straight-cut bit to rout for the back panel to fit the sides. A test piece compared with the cross stretcher helps to check the fit (see photos 4, 5).

Rout the back edge of the carcass sides with a 45° chamfering bit. Then, with the same bit, rout the front and sides of the top and bottom. Cut the ¼" birch plywood back panel to fit.

Sand the carcass parts through a range of grits. Use an orbital sander for the flat surfaces, and to avoid unnecessary rounding, a sanding block on the chamfered edges.

Make the Turnings and Doors

Use the same techniques as used for making the lids for the Half-Turned Box. Again, I use the indexing pins on the plywood faceplate to locate and secure the halves to the cast-iron faceplate on the lathe. For the Pin Cabinet, because the doors are larger, I also use wood screws through the back of the plywood faceplate into the sassafras workpieces. The holes will be plugged and sanded after completion.

Turn the pieces to a pleasing shape, and sand them while still on the lathe. To make the turnings reflect the shape of the intersection of the doors when closed, cut away a greater depth at the center. Remove the turnings; fill and plug the attachment points, and sand the back side.

Cut the doors to half the width of the carcass, then using the jointer, finish the sawn edge by removing about ⅓₂" for clearance when opening and closing.

Rout the inside and outside edges. I used a larger-diameter roundover bit on the inside edge to reflect the shape of the turning, but a smaller roundover bit on the outside to avoid cutting into the space required for the barrel-hinge holes to be drilled.

Make the Hangers

Cut the hanger parts to size, then use the ³⁄₁₆" straight-cut bit in the router table to cut the mortises into the vertical pieces. Adjust the fence to position the cut. I use an extralong fence to allow stop blocks to be used for controlling the workpiece and the length of the mortise. Note that the mortises are off center so the horizontal hangers don't lie flush against the inside of the doors, allowing clearance for necklaces to hang on the doors. Cut the mortises in steps to ease the cut and avoid breaking the router bit (see photo 6).

Cut the tenons on the horizontal pieces, using the sled on the table saw. Cut the shoulders first, then, turning the pieces vertically, trim the tenons to size to fit the mortises (see photo 7). I use a small accessory made for the sled to give better vertical support to the workpieces while the tenons are being cut. Cut the ends and one side of the tenon on the first setup, then adjust the stop block for the final cut, keeping the face side against the stop block (see photos 8 & 9). Use a piece of scrap to test the exact sizing of the tenon to the mortise. This gives you a chance to double-check the setup before cutting the actual part.

Use a rasp to round the corners of the tenons to fit the mortises (see photo 10). Cut the horizontal parts to the final length and angle.

Use a ⅛" roundover bit in the router table to round the edges of the hanger parts. Then sand the hanger parts using an orbital sander.

Hinge the Doors and Hangers

Both the doors and hangers are hinged with barrel hinges: 14mm hinges for the doors and 10mm for the hanger assemblies.

First, drill 14mm holes in the cabinet sides and door edges. This will take two separate setups, requiring changes in the drill depth setting. You can use stops with the fence to control the position of the holes or simply mark in pencil where you want to drill. Align carefully before drilling. Again, if you choose to set up stops along the fence to position the holes, an index piece will help in aligning the opposite holes. Drill the holes in the cabinet sides with the sides standing vertically against the fence. Then drill the holes in the doors with the doors flat on the drill table.

Drill 10mm holes into the vertical hangers, and matching holes into the outside edges of the doors. Note that for the smaller hinges, the fence location and drill depth will need to be changed to allow for the reduced clearance in the opening of the hinge.

Ebonize the Cherry Parts

Ebonizing is a very old way to color wood and is effective on a number of domestic hardwoods. Ebonizing is a chemical reaction in which iron, in a mild acid solution, reacts with tannins in the wood, turning them black or gray. The depth of color possible depends on the amount of tannin available in the wood and the amount of

8 **Cut one side of the tenon.**

9 **Reposition the fence to cut the other side of the tenon, keeping the face side against the stop block.**

10 **Use a rasp to round the corners of the tenons. On small tenons like these, a few quick strokes will do the job.**

iron delivered to it. In my experience, it is always risky and experimental: often two pieces of the same species will react differently to the treatment. Before deciding to ebonize wood, test a sample and be prepared for unexpected results.

Dissolve 0000 steel wool in vinegar. Cheap white vinegar will do. Nails, or any other source of iron will work, but steel wool gives the most immediate results. Wait about 24 hours for the formula to become effective.

Brush the solution onto the wood. Avoid getting it into the biscuit slots (see photo 11). The solution doesn't seem to affect the adherence of glue, but I don't want it to puddle, which would result in longer drying time. The wood will darken as it dries.

Depending on the wood, it may take two or even three applications to reach the depth of black desired. I look for a nice contrast between the ebonized cherry and the sassafras. Light sanding with 320-grit paper between coats will smooth the grain that has been raised through wetting the wood.

Prepare for Assembly

Apply the Danish oil finish to all of the parts prior to assembly. Be careful to avoid getting oil into the slots for the biscuits because oil will interfere with the effectiveness of the glue.

Drill the bottom of the cabinet for the bullet catches to fit (see photo 12). To accurately locate the position of each hole, measure to the center point of the bullet cup, adding 1/32" for clearance, plus the width of the sides. Set up the fence and stop blocks to drill the holes, or simply mark their positions, and drill to the required depth.

To drill for the bullet cups to fit the doors, use a 1/2" drill bit and a doweling jig with a handheld electric drill (see photo 13). Set the depth stop so as not to go too deep. To check the depth, I drilled a test piece using a cutoff from the final cutting of the doors. As with most woodworking processes, there are many alternative approaches to this operation.

11 Use steel wool dissolved in vinegar to ebonize the cabinet parts. The solution brushes on clear but quickly turns gray and ultimately black with additional applications.

12 Drill for the bullet catches to fit prior to assembly.

13 Use a doweling jig and handheld drill to drill for the catch cups to fit the doors.

Assemble the Cabinet

Use biscuits to join the sides to the cross stretcher, carefully aligning the sides to the top of the stretcher. Then put the back panel in place.

Use biscuits to join the bottom, and then the top, to the sides and cross stretcher. Use clamps to hold the parts together while the glue dries (see photo 14). Carefully measure corner to corner on the cabinet to make certain it's square. If it isn't, loosen the clamps slightly, adjust it and retighten.

After the cabinet is assembled, attach the turnings to the top and bottom. Use the biscuit joiner to establish the mounting positions. I preferred not to glue the turned pieces in place, and instead drilled black screws from inside the cabinet to firmly attach them.

Make the Internal Parts

Mark the positions on the doors for the brass necklace hangers, and drill the angled holes for them to fit. Then cut frame stock at an angle for stretching fabric (the angle provides clearance for hanging pins and earrings).

Miter the corners of the frame stock. Use the miter sled on the table saw to insure close tolerances. Glue and screw or nail the frame together.

After the back frame is covered with fabric, it can be screwed in place from the back. Sew material to cover the door hangers, then install the hinges in the doors and wings.

Hanging Instructions

Determine where you want to place the cabinet. Make a pencil mark at the top center of the location on the wall. Measure down 3½" and make another mark. Using a level on the bottom of the hanger strip, hold it level and in alignment with the pencil mark.

Drill a hole through the hanger strip into a stud if possible. Countersink the screw hole. Tighten a screw in place. You may want to use a molly or wall anchor. Put in another screw on the opposite side of the hanger strip to keep the cabinet from tilting on the wall. Lift the cabinet in place.

14 Use bar clamps to assemble the cabinet after gluing. Note how the pads are used to prevent marring the finished cabinet parts. Don't forget to check the cabinet for square.

Intentional Imperfection

Many cultures around the world share an interesting notion of perfection. Amish quilt makers would leave a single stitch undone rather than make the "perfect" quilt, expressing their belief that only God could make something perfect. Among weavers in Turkey, the same idea is found. Many Chinese and Japanese artists believe that their work should include "incompleteness and imperfection," an "emptiness" that leaves room for further growth.

I've never had much problem with perfection. I've yet to make the perfect box or the perfect piece of furniture. I can't imagine in my own work the need to leave something imperfect as a statement, to ever complete the "perfect" piece and find myself in that predicament. A craftsman sees the points where his or her own work needs refinement—the little slips of the saw or chisel, the sanding marks, the slight rounding where something should be straight. Fortunately, most observers don't notice these things and accept our work, seeing it as perfect despite its many flaws, or at least, choosing to pay attention to its strengths.

In woodworking, we face the inevitable. As human beings and not machines, we make mistakes in measuring. Things slip both from the fingers and from the mind as we work. Wood is not the perfect material. It has imperfections. It is always expanding and contracting in response to changes in climate, challenging the artist in his efforts to make the "perfect" piece.

A gentleman I once met is friends with the famous rocking chair maker, Sam Maloof. The gentleman told me the following story. Sam was visiting Japan and was shown a beautiful storage box for sweaters. He noted how precisely it was made and marveled to his hosts that something could be made of real wood to such close tolerances. He asked, "Doesn't this lid swell shut in the humid summer months?" His hosts answered, "Yes, but it is a sweater box. Who would open it then?"

As we develop our skills through new projects, our ideas about "perfection" evolve. Perfection is elusive, always just beyond our reach like the carrot on the stick.

I am lucky to live in a community that has encouraged my work with wood. I often go into friends' homes and find work that I had done years ago when my skills were not as well developed. I can look at each piece from a critical perspective, finding fault with my earlier shortcomings, or I can find in each piece some small steps that were taken in my personal growth as a woodworker and feel honored that the work is cherished and loved despite its flaws.

Growth toward "perfection" is part of the story that woodworking tells. When you begin to understand that woodworking is storytelling, each "slip" of the chisel becomes part of the "perfection" of the finished piece. With this in mind, you have no reason not to begin making boxes.

Chapter 10

Cherry Jewelry Chest

Sometimes I find certain boards irresistible, even though I may have no idea right then as to how I'll use the wood. The cherry panel in the top of this box is from such a board. The interesting figuring is from burls forming on the surface of the tree.

This box is made with an unhinged lid that simply pivots and drops into a recess to hold it in the open position, and then closes with a slight lift on the pull, thus eliminating the need for expensive hinges and lid supports. The ebonized walnut pull, the raised trim strip and the feet are chemically treated to attain their rich black color prior to final assembly.

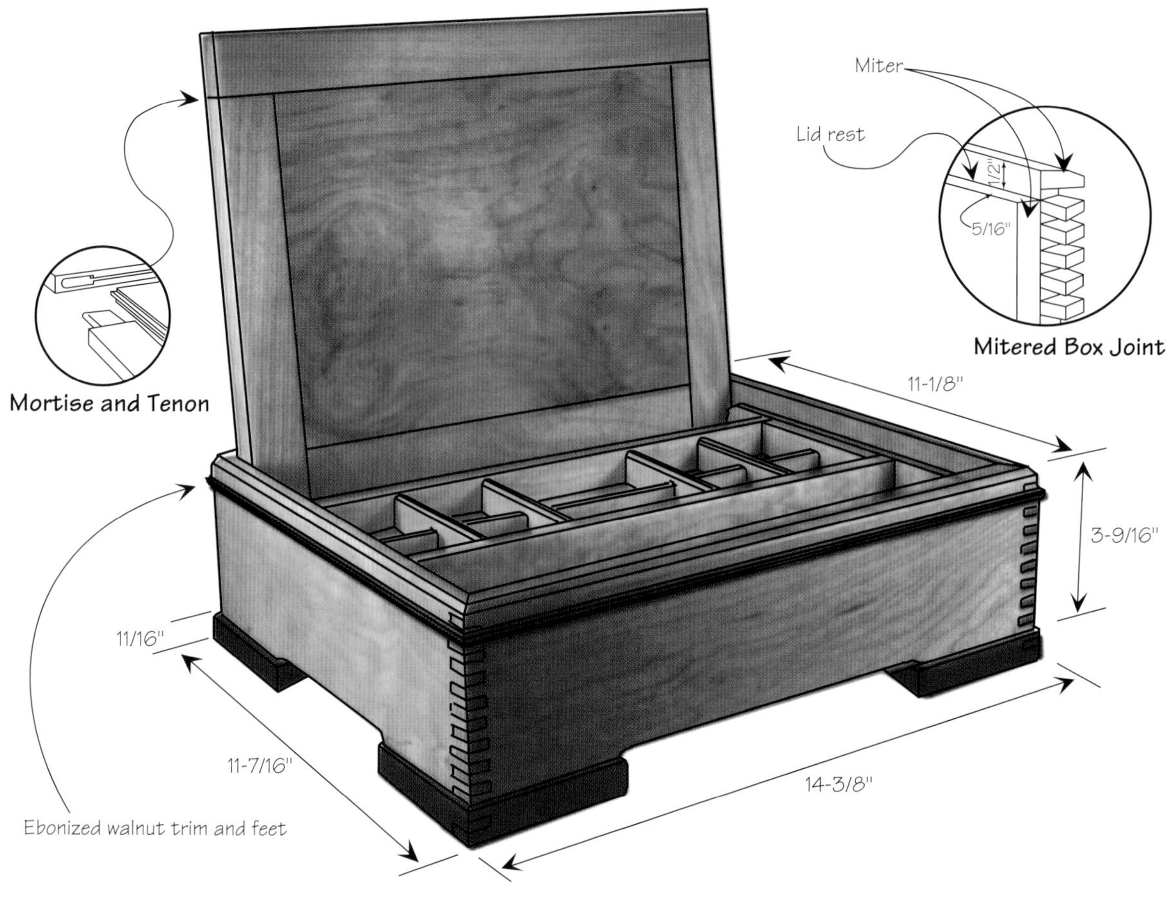

Bill of Materials

PART NAME	NUMBER	DIMENSION TWL	COMMENTS
Sides	2	3/4 x 3 9/16 x 11 3/16	
Front	2	3/4 x 3 9/16 x 14 1/16	
Back	2	3/4 x 3 9/16 x 14 1/16	
Bottom	1	1/4 x 10 x 13	Baltic birch plywood
Lid Sides	2	5/8 x 1 1/4 x 9 3/4	
Lid Front	1	5/8 x 1 1/4 x 13 1/8	
Lid Back	1	5/8 x 1 1/4 x 12 1/16	
Lid Panel	1	5/8 x 8 1/8 x 11 1/32	
Feet	4	13/16 x 15/16 x 8	Cut to size after gluing
Tray Ends	2	5/16 x 1 1/8 x 4 5/16	
Tray Front	1	5/16 x 1 1/8 x 12 1/16	Includes 1/8" tenons
Tray Back	1	5/16 x 1 1/8 x 12 1/16	Includes 1/8" tenons
Tray Bottom	1	1/8 x 4 1/16 x 12 1/32	Baltic birch plywood
Tray Divider	1	5/16 x 1/2 x 11 13/16	
Tray Dividers	3 or 4	5/16 x 3/4 x 3 13/16	
Box Dividers	2	5/16 x 1 x 12 1/2	
Box Dividers	3	5/16 x 1 1/4 x 9 5/8	
Tray Guides	2	3/16 x 3/8 x 9 5/8	
Trim Strips	2	3/16 x 3/4 x 27	Cut to size after ebonizing and finish

Cut the Finger Joints

Set the cut height of the finger joint jig to 7/16" to allow for a small amount to be sanded flush after assembly. Use a 3/16" spiral cutter and cut an index piece to fit over the stop pin. Clamp the index piece in place and make the first cuts in the bottom corners of the end pieces. Then remove the index piece from the jig and make all the cuts in the ends, front and back. Hold the workpiece tight to the pin, stepping over it to align for each consecutive cut. The last cut on each piece will be cut at a miter on the table saw.

Use the miter sled on the table saw to cut the mitered corners at the top of the box. Follow the steps shown in making the Bracelet Box.

Trim the fingers to width on the table saw. Stand the box sides on end and pass them between the saw blade and fence. Set the fence to leave 7/16",

1 **Use a template and a pattern maker's bit to rout the clearance in the sides for the lid to open.**

2 **Use a squeeze bottle to apply glue to the fingers as the box is assembled.**

3 **If the measurements are the same from corner to corner both ways, it is square.**

4 **Cut the tenons for the box lid on the table saw.**

and set the blade to the same height as the router bit in the finger joint jig.

Using the mitered cutoff sled on the table saw, tilt the arbor to 45°. Control the position of the cut with a stop block, and trim the excess from around the finger joints.

On the table saw, cut the lip on the box front and sides to provide the frame around the lid. Stand the sides up along the fence to make the first cut, leaving 7⁄16" remaining of the box side and cutting about 5⁄8" deep so that the 3⁄4"-thick lid will stand proud. Next, adjust the fence and saw blade height to cut away the stock from the inside of the front and sides. Perform the same steps on the inside back of the box, but make the first cut 13⁄8" deep to allow for the lid to rest in an open position.

To rout the box sides to provide lid clearance, make a template the same size as the box side from scrap wood. Make a 7⁄8" × 13⁄8" cut out of one corner, with the 7⁄8" being measured from the end of the stock. Clamp this template over the box side and, with the mortise cleanup bit set to the same depth as the rabbet on the side, rout the recess for the lid (see photo 1).

Before assembly, rout for the box bottom and drawer guides to fit. Sand the inside surfaces of the sides, front, back and bottom. Be sure to check the box for being square as you glue, assemble and clamp it together (see photos 2, 3).

Make the Lid

Plane or sand the panel to thickness. Use a drum sander to avoid tear-out of the burl pattern.

After cutting the panel-frame parts to size, mortise both ends of the front piece and one end on each of the two side pieces with a 1⁄4" straight-cut bit in the router table. Set up stops to control the length of cut, and make the cut to full depth by gradually raising the height of the cutter over a series of steps. Mark a face side on the stock, and make all cuts with the face side against the fence.

Cut the tenons on the back frame piece and on one end of each side piece. First trim the shoulders of the stock, and then using either a tenoning

5 Use the router table and ¼" straight cut bit to rout the dadoes for the top panel to fit.

6 Use the router table and fence to form the trim strips. Use the 45° chamfering bit first to give it shape, then a straight-cut router bit to cut it to fit the channel in the box.

jig on the table saw or a stop block as shown in the photos, stand the pieces on end and shape the tenons. Index each piece with the face side against either the stop block or the tenoning jig to maintain accuracy (see photo 4). Use a rasp to trim the shoulders of the tenons to fit the mortises, and a chisel to trim in the corners for a final fit.

Test fit the frame parts together. Take careful measurement for cutting the panel to size. Add to the dimensions of the opening ½" in each direction for the ¼" tongues, but subtract about 1/16" in width and about 1/32" in length to allow for wood movement.

With the top frame assembled, use the 45° chamfering bit to rout the inside edges of the frame. Then using a chisel, finish the cut into the corners.

Cut dadoes in the frame parts for the panel to fit. Rout so that the dadoes end in the mortises. Stop blocks can be used, or simply lower the workpiece so the router bit enters the mortise at the opposite end (see photo 5).

Make a relief cut using the table saw, and then, using the 1" straight-cut bit, rout the tongues in the panel edges. Check the fit in the dadoes cut for the frame.

Use the 45° chamfering bit on edges of the panel where it will intersect the frame. Sand the chamfers on the panel and frame parts. After putting glue into the mortises, assemble the panel and frame and clamp them together. Measure corner to corner on the frame and panel assembly to check for square.

Make the Trim

Plane some walnut stock down to ⅞" thick and then rip 5/16" strips from it. Use the sanding disk in the table saw to thickness the stock to ¼". Set up the router table and fence with the 45° chamfering bit, and chamfer each edge of the walnut strips (see photo 6). Then change to a straight-cut bit and rout channels in each side of the walnut strips. Check the thickness of the remaining wood at the center of the strip to see that it measures ⅛".

Sand each edge of the walnut strips, then ebonize them with a vinegar-and-steel-wool solution. When the strips have dried, rub them with steel wool or lightly sand and treat again. Once the strips have reached the desired color, smooth them again with steel wool and finish them with Danish oil.

Install the Trim

Install a ⅛" bit in the router table, adjusting the fence so that the cut will hit right in the middle of one of the fingers of the finger joints. On my box, I adjusted the fence to measure from the outside of the cut. With the bottom of the box against the fence, rout each side in turn to cut the channel for the trim strips to fit.

On the table saw, cut the individual trim strips free. Set the fence so that the tongues remaining on the strips equal the depth of the channels routed for them to fit. In the event that the strips are too tight, widen the distance between the cutter and the fence, and rout the box sides again, slightly widening the channel.

Using the mitered cutoff sled, cut the trim pieces to length. Wait until the body of the box has been sanded and finished with Danish oil before gluing the strips in place.

Make the Feet

The feet are made using the same techniques used for making the box sides. If you wish to duplicate this box exactly, you will find it helpful to make the feet at the same time as making the box front, back and sides.

After cutting the stock to length, use the box-joint jig and router to cut the finger joints. Follow the same procedure as used for the box sides. Cut the corner stock parts to equal lengths. Plan for some waste when the corners are cut to length. Then cut the inside miters, as with the box sides, and then miter the top corners.

Glue and assemble the sides to form a single unit that will be cut into four corners after the glue has dried. Use the belt and disc sander to clean up the corners, sanding the joints flush.

Use the table saw with the arbor tilted 10° to cut the corners free from the assembled unit. Chamfer the edges, then sand, ebonize and finish with Danish oil using the same techniques as for making the trim strips. Finally, drill and countersink the bottoms of the feet for attaching to the box.

Make the Pull

Make the pull from walnut using the same tenoning technique as used for making the pull for the Men's Jewelry Box. Use the table saw with the arbor tilted to define its shape. I chose a more geometric shape to go with the inward angle chosen for the feet (see photo 7). Ebonize and finish the pulls to match the feet and trim strips.

Make the Trays

Mortise the end pieces. Use the same technique on the router table as for the Inlaid Walnut Ring Box. Tenon the front and back pieces using the same technique used for making the tenons in the Inlaid Walnut Ring Box. The ⅛" mortises and tenons are adequate for this task (see photo 8).

Rout between mortises for the tray bottom to fit. Using a ⅛" kerfed blade in the table saw, cut the dado for the box bottom, so that it will align with the dado cuts in the tray ends.

Using the cutoff sled on the table saw, adjust the blade height to cut through the nubs left on the back and front of the tray. Set the stop block on the fence to position the cut. Trim off the nubs flush with the tenon shoulders. Then rout the edges of the box parts, sand the interior surface and then assemble the trays.

Make the Dividers

I chose to have removable dividers, which allow the box to be lined before the dividers are put in place. The dividers use a half-overlap system for their parts to be joined and positioned. In order to give a more finished look to the assembled dividers, I use taller stock for the pieces moving one direction than the other. This allows for the edges to be routed smooth.

Using a ¼" dado blade and the cutoff sled on the table saw, make a crosscut on a piece of scrap stock. As the

7 Use the table saw, miter slide and stop block to shape the pulls. I first trimmed the ends to shape and then the sides.

8 After tenoning the tray parts, the perfect fit is shown when despite gravity and no glue, the parts hold together.

9 Use a dado blade in the table saw to cut the lap joints for the divider parts.

scrap stock is milled to thickness, use it to check the thickness of stock for the dividers (see photo 9).

Set the dado blade to half the height of the narrower stock, and clamp a stop block in place on the sled to locate the position for the dado cut. Change the location of the stop block to position other cuts, using the same technique to dado the matching pieces.

Rout the edges of the parts prior to assembly with a 45° chamfering bit. This narrows the strips, making them appear thinner. Sand and finish the parts with Danish oil before gluing together.

The Joy of Doing Without

We, as woodworkers, are frequently fooled into believing that some whatsit is needed, when perhaps our souls crave the experience of learning to do without. We live in a highly technological age, but many of us are called toward a simpler relationship with wood, using hand tools wherever possible and finding greater pleasure and satisfaction in the process of work than in the accomplishment of finished products. It is easy to be led by television woodworking or even by the pages of this book to think that certain equipment will be necessary to do woodworking, and yet many woodworkers make a conscious effort to rely on their personal inventiveness and take great pleasure in sustaining traditional techniques.

As a "professional" woodworker, I've always been so close on the cash flow that I seldom have the money to buy new tools. So I make do with what I have and reap the benefit of discovering my own inventiveness and creativity. My favorite tools are actually the oldest ones in my shop. They are like very old friends. That old song line, "Make new friends, but keep the old; one is silver and the other gold," is as true of our tools as of the people in our lives.

I try to keep a balance in my work between the pleasure I derive from it and the efficiency necessary to survive as a "professional." This balance is something that all of us face as woodworkers. We may have slightly impatient spouses who wonder what's taking so long in the shop. We may be having to justify in our own minds the expense of tools and materials when we perhaps started out with the delusions of "saving" money while furnishing our homes.

I think the answer to much of this is to savor the moment—realize there is a balance to be sought somewhere between the fully equipped shop and the something-from-nothing approach. The point of balance is unique for each of us. We need not respond like robots to the latest tool or technique. Cherish the inefficiencies of the old and the history it holds dear. Find satisfaction and pleasure in doing without and find new and wonderful levels of inventiveness, creativity and satisfaction in our woodworking lives.

Chapter 11

Lucy's Jewelry Box

My daughter, Lucy, is a box collector. She's saved many old reject boxes from my workshop scrap pile. It doesn't matter to her whether they are chipped, scratched, broken or still rough unfinished wood; if they're capable of holding some small treasure, they're worth saving. This jewelry box is one I made for her ninth birthday. It is made from pecan and walnut with a small inlaid window of curly maple. It has a drawer at the bottom and an interior tray that lifts as the lid is opened. The pecan was some rough-sawn 5/4 lumber from Texas that a friend sold to me. I was able to resaw it to get ½" planed sides for the box and ⅜" bookmatched panels for the top.

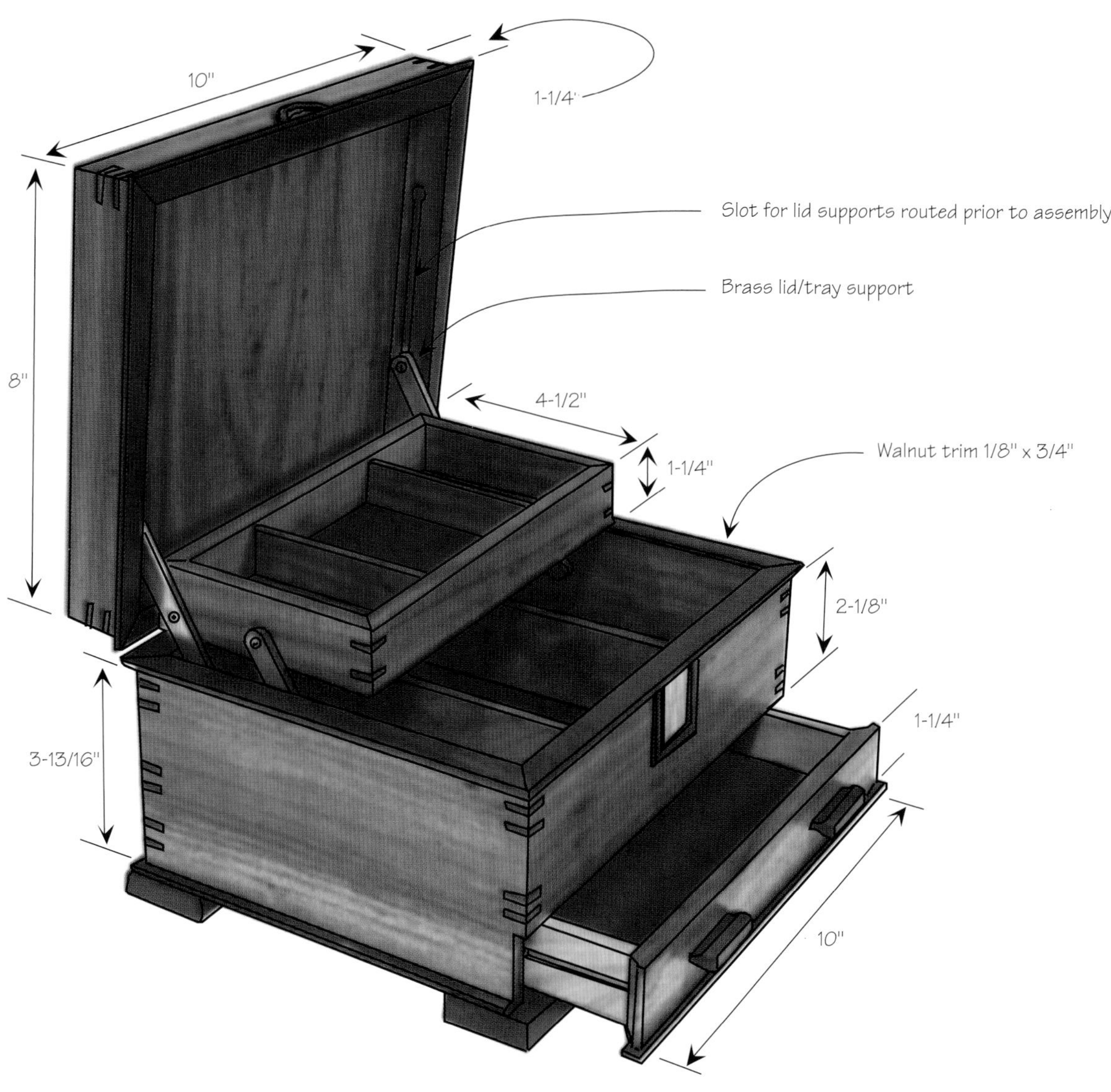

Overview

This is one of the more complicated boxes in the book and one that I suggest for more advanced woodworkers who may already have some understanding of the sequence of steps required. Many of the techniques used are covered in other projects. The following is an overview of making Lucy's Jewelry Box, with some of the steps left out because of space requirements.

Making the Box

After planing the material to thickness, rip the stock to width, leaving it wide enough to allow for the saw kerf width that will be required for cutting the drawer apart from the front (see photo 1). Select the piece of wood that will be the front of the box, and cut away the lower portion. This lower portion will become the drawer front. Use the table saw to cut the dadoes in the front, back and sides to allow for the top panel, box bottom and drawer guides.

Tilt the saw arbor to 45° and use the 45° angled sled to cut the box sides, front and back to the required lengths (see photo 2). Rip saw the box sides, front and back to about 1⁄32" over finished dimension, and then use the jointer to bring the parts to finished size.

With a 3⁄16" bit in the router table, and using stop blocks to control the movement of the box front and back along the fence, rout for the interior dividers to fit. Use the table saw to cut away the front lower portions of the box sides where the drawer front will fit.

Make the Tray Lifters/ Lid Supports

In making this box, it's helpful to create a working model of the relationships between parts to help locate the exact positions for holes to be drilled and slots to be cut. I made my model from bits and pieces of scrap Masonite (see

Bill of Materials

PART NAME	NUMBER	DIMENSION TWL	COMMENTS
Front	1	½ x 5½ x 10	Allows for saw kerf to cut drawer front
Back	1	½ x 5¼ x 10	
Sides	2	½ x 5¼ x 8	
Top panel	1	½ x 7⅜ x 9⅜	Includes 3⁄16" tongues on panel
Bottom	1	7⅜ x 9⅜	⅛" Baltic birch plywood
Dividers	2	3⁄16 x 1¾ x 7¼	
Feet	4	½ x 1⅝ x 1⅝	
Tray			
Sides	2	⅜ x 1¼ x 4½	
Front and Back	2	⅜ x 1¼ x 8⅝	
Dividers	2	⅛ x ¾ x 4	
Bottom	1	4 x 8⅛	⅛" Baltic birch plywood
Drawer			
Sides	2	5⁄16" x 1¼" x 7 7⁄32"	Includes 3⁄16" tenon
Back	1	5⁄16" x 1¼" x 8¾"	Includes 3⁄16" tenons at each end
Front (cut from front of box)		½" x 1¼" x 10"	
Bottom	1	⅛" x 6 15⁄16" x 8⅝"	Baltic birch plywood
Tray Lift Mechanism			
Front Lift Arms	2	3⁄16" x ½" x 2½"	
Back Lift Arms	2	3⁄16" x ½" x 4½"	From 1⁄16" brass sheet stock
Screws and Nuts	2	8nc32 x ½" long	Flat head brass
Brass Screws	8	#4 x ½" long	Flat head
Hardware and Supplies			
Screws	6	1¼" #6	Flat head
Curly maple and walnut stock for inlay.			
⅛" walnut stock for trim			
⅛" x ½" stock walnut stock for slip feathers			
5⁄16" x 1¼" walnut stock for drawer pulls.			

photo 3). In making the model, the parts should be sized to correspond to the end view of the lid and box sides after the saw kerf is subtracted in separating the lid from the base. Also allow for the ⅛" walnut bandings that will be added to the edges.

Using a keyhole bit, rout in the box side for the screw to attach the lift mechanism. Use the fence and stop blocks to control the length and position of the cut (see photo 4). Use the model to determine the locations inside the box for the mechanism to fit, and drill the pilot holes before the box is assembled (see photo 5).

Make the small lift parts using the model to determine the lengths. Make the rear lifters from three layers of sheet brass. Use an old carbide blade in the table saw to cut the brass, then round the corners on a belt sander before polishing.

Make the Panel Top

Resaw enough pecan to form the top panel and plane it to thickness. Joint and glue the panels to achieve the full width required (it's good to make a relief cut with the table saw to ease the router's work by reducing the router's pull on the workpiece). After forming the panel, use a 1⁄16" roundover bit to shape its edge, and to soften the edge of the box sides where the panel will intersect (see photos 6, 7).

1 To make efficient use of material, resaw the material for the sides from thicker stock. This process also gives better opportunity to match grains and color of wood.

2 Use the miter sled on the table saw to cut the miters at the corners of the box. Use a stop block clamped to the fence to control the lengths of the parts.

3 Build a model of the tray lift mechanism. This will help for understanding the relationship between parts and be useful in setting up to mill the actual parts.

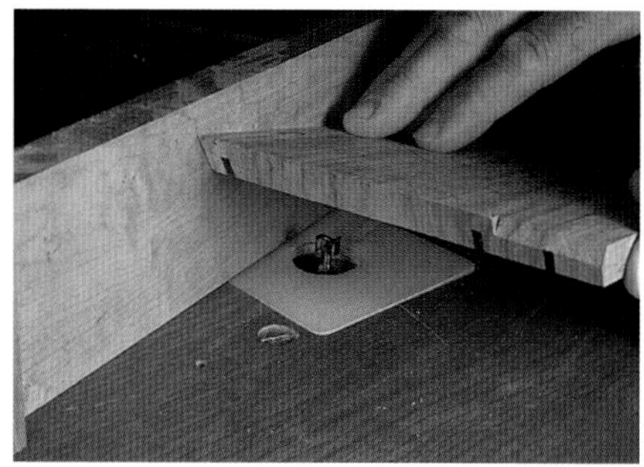

4 Use a key hole router bit to route in the box side for the tray lift mechanism to fit, using the parts from the model as a guide for set-up.

5 Use the model for setting up to drill the box sides for the lift mechanism to fit. This needs to be done before the box is assembled.

6 Use the router table to cut the tongues on the panel top. Note the relief cut made on the table saw prior to routing. Use a 1" straight cut router bit, and clamp safety blocking securely in place to protect your fingers.

7 Use a 1⁄8" round over bit in the router table to shape the edges of the panel. I raise the height of the router bit above the table to allow for the tongue on the panel. Lower the bit before routing the matching roundover on the inside edges of the box sides.

8 Spread glue on the miters before assembly. The raised panel should not be glued in place.

9 Use band clamps to hold the box parts in position as the glue sets. Check that the box is square before the glue dries. This can be done either with a small square or by measuring from corner to corner.

Assemble the Box

After sanding the inside surfaces of the box sides, front, back, top panel, bottom and dividers, apply glue to the mitered surfaces and use band clamps to hold the miters closed tightly until the glue sets (see photo 8). Be sure to put the internal dividers in place as the box is assembled. Use a spacer block at the bottom front of the box to keep the box from squeezing in where the drawer will fit (see photo 9). After the glue has fully dried, use the slip feather jig on the router table to cut for the walnut corner splines to fit (see photo 10). Place the walnut slip feathers into the corners using glue to lock them in place. Sand the splines flush with the surrounding surface of the box.

Make the Inlay Templates

Making and inlaying the parts for the front of the box requires making three templates and using the inlay guide

10 Use the slip-feather jig on the router table to cut the box corners for the slip feathers to fit. The block of wood resting in the V positions the cut.

11 Use the mortise cleanup router bit in the router table to form the template for inlaying the front of the box. The underlying template used to guide the cut is made by drilling a hole in a piece of plywood, cutting into it from the edge using the table saw, then nailing this piece and a small filler block in place on the workpiece.

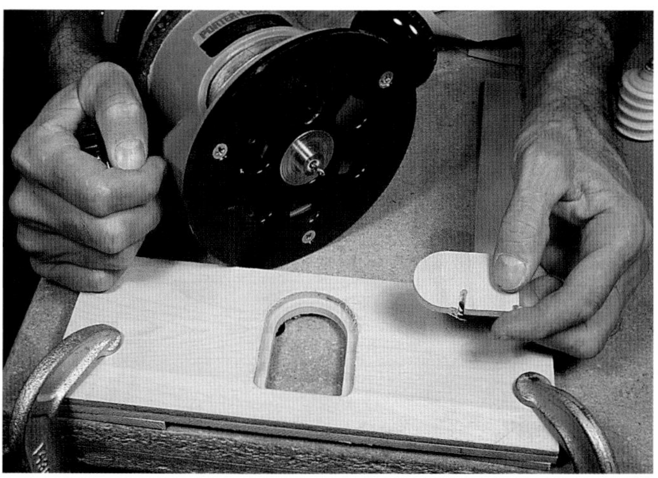

12 Use the first template to guide in making the second. Using the inlay guide-bushing set with the brass bushing in place creates an offset template smaller than the first.

13 Use the larger template to rout the front of the box for the inlay to fit. Start by lowering the cutter into the stock, then follow the perimeter of the template before removing the waste.

bushing set used for the Wedding Ring Music Box. The primary template is used to form the working templates for shaping and inlaying the parts.

First, drill a hole in plywood stock the same size as the box front for ease of alignment when installing the inlay. Drill a hole larger than the planned inlay, and using the table saw, cut into the circle from the edge of the stock to form the oblong squared shape. Replace the lower portion of the cut with a piece of plywood to close the shape, and attach these with brads to a second piece of plywood of the same size.

Place the template and the shape beneath it over a template-following bit in your router table. Following the guide bearing, cut the shape of the first working template in the template stock (see photo 11). Separate the template from the initial forms and attach the new working template to another piece of plywood of the same size. Then using the inlay guide bushing set, route the second template using the first working template to determine its shape and size (see photo 12). Using the guide bushing set creates a second template smaller in size that the original.

Inlay the Front

This procedure is the same as used for making the Triangle Ring Box except that the templates are clamped in place. Clamp the first template in place over the front of the box. Then use the router, ⅛" router bit and guide bushing with the brass bushing in place (see photo 13). Set the depth of cut to about $\frac{1}{16}$". Test on a piece of scrap, and use the dial caliper to check depth. Remove all the material inside the space defined by the template with your router.

Remove the brass bushing and adjust the depth of cut. Then clamp the template in place over a piece of walnut. Use double-stick carpet tape to firmly attach the walnut to some scrap stock so it doesn't shift during the routing operations (see photo 14).

14 **Use these two template to cut the parts for inlay. I use carpet tape to adhere the inlay stock to a piece of scrap wood, then clamp the template in place. Inside shapes are routed with the brass bushing in place. Outside shapes are routed with the brass bushing removed.**

15 **After the inlay space is defined on the box, use the table saw to cut the lid from the body of the box. Use shims to keep the box parts in position so they will not bind on the blade.**

16 **Use the router table with fence and 3⁄16" straight cut router bit to cut the mortises in the drawer sides and front. Move the work piece between the stops clamped to the fence.**

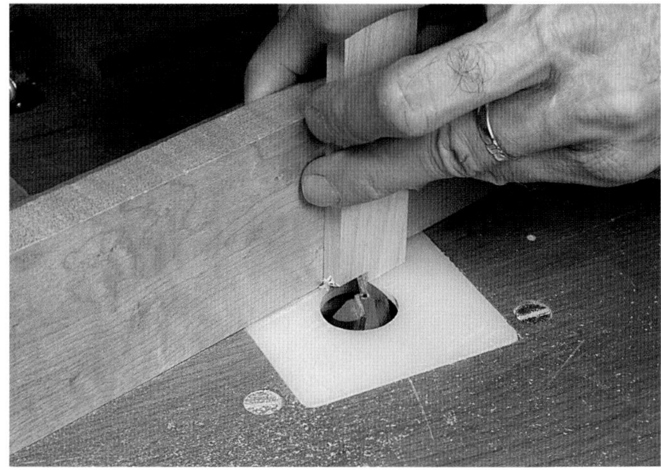

17 **Cut the tenons for the drawer sides and back on the router table with a 1" straight-cut router bit.**

Install the brass bushing to the guide bushing. Clamp the template with the smaller opening over the walnut stock and rout to cut away the inside of the piece. Clamp the smaller template over a piece of curly maple taped to scrap stock and, after removing the bushing, rout the maple piece.

Route the edges of the walnut piece and hand sand it to prepare it for inlaying. Cut the inlay pieces apart and glue them in place after the lid is cut from the box. Use the table saw to cut the lid away from the base of the box, replacing the saw kerf with shims to keep the box from closing on the blade (see photo 15).

Make the Drawer

The drawers are made using mortise-and-tenon joints like when making the Inlaid Ring Box. First, cut the drawer to fit the shape of the front of the box. Use the 1⁄8" router bit in the router table to rout mortises in the drawer front for the sides to fit (see photo 16). Change the position of the fence and stops to rout mortises into the drawer sides for the tenons on the drawer back to fit.

With a 1" straight-cut bit, rout tenons on the drawer back and sides. Check the fits in the mortise and adjust if necessary (see photo 17).

Using the sled on the table saw, trim nubs away from the tenons to make

18 **After trimming the tenons to width using the table saw sled, the drawer can be trial-assembled.**

19 Use the miter sled to trim the drawer front to fit the sides of the box. The stop block controls the position of the cut and the blade height is lowered to allow for the overlap at the front of the box.

20 Use the router table to cut the mortises in the tray front and back for dividers to fit. I use a ⅛" straight cut router bit. Note the dado cut for the tray bottom to fit.

them the same width as the mortises (see photo 18). Rout the sides, front and back for the drawer bottom to fit. Route for the drawer pulls to fit. Prior to assembly, cut the drawer face to match the shape of the box front using the miter cutoff sled (see photo 19).

Make the Drawer Pulls

Unlike the pull used in the Men's Jewelry Box, the drawer pulls used here are routed with a roundover bit for their final shaping rather than a chamfering bit (see the instructions for making the Men's Jewelry Box for the proper technique).

Make the Tray

Cut the miters for the tray using the miter cutoff sled on the table saw. Then before assembly, rout the slots for the dividers and for the tray bottom to fit (see photo 20). Apply glue to the corners and fit the dividers and bottom in place as the tray is assembled. Use the slip-feather jig on the router table to rout for the slip feathers to fit.

Attach the Walnut Trim

Hand sand the inlay parts before fitting them into the box front. They should be sanded before the final cutting and gluing in place (see photo 21). Use a brad nailer and glue to attach the walnut trim strips. Miter them to fit the corners, and carefully fit them to the bottom of the drawer front and bottom of the box (see photo 22). Cut walnut feet and attach them with wood screws and clear adhesive. You will need to cut a small relief space on the front feet to provide clearance for the drawer to slide without scraping.

As with all the other boxes, sand through a range of grits up to about 320 and then use Danish oil to finish. After oiling, install the interior tray, lift mechanism and lid support. To attach it to the lid, use a flathead brass screw and nut tapped into the brass lift mechanism (see photos 23, 24).

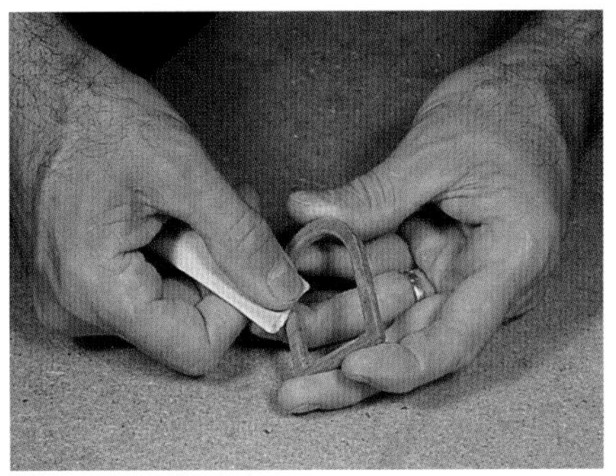

21 Hand sand the inlay parts before final fitting to the box lid and body. Use the table saw and sled to cut the parts to final size.

22 Miter the walnut trim pieces to fit the lid and box body. I use a brad nailer and glue to attach the trim strips.

23 Use a tap to cut threads in the brass supports to hold the screws in place.

24 Check the operation of the tray lift before installing the lid (one brass support arm will have to be removed and replaced as the lid is attached).

Chapter 12

Ash Chest of Drawers

This chest of drawers is made with wood originally harvested from the White River Valley in northwest Arkansas as Beaver Lake was constructed by the U.S. Army Corps of Engineers in the 1950s. The densely figured wood was then used as a kitchen countertop in my home. After nearly twenty years of use, the 2¼" slab of solid ash had badly warped. When we replaced the countertop, the thick slab of ash was put away in my shop while my imagination was stirring. How could I make use of this beautiful piece of wood? Now in the wood's new life, it is a box.

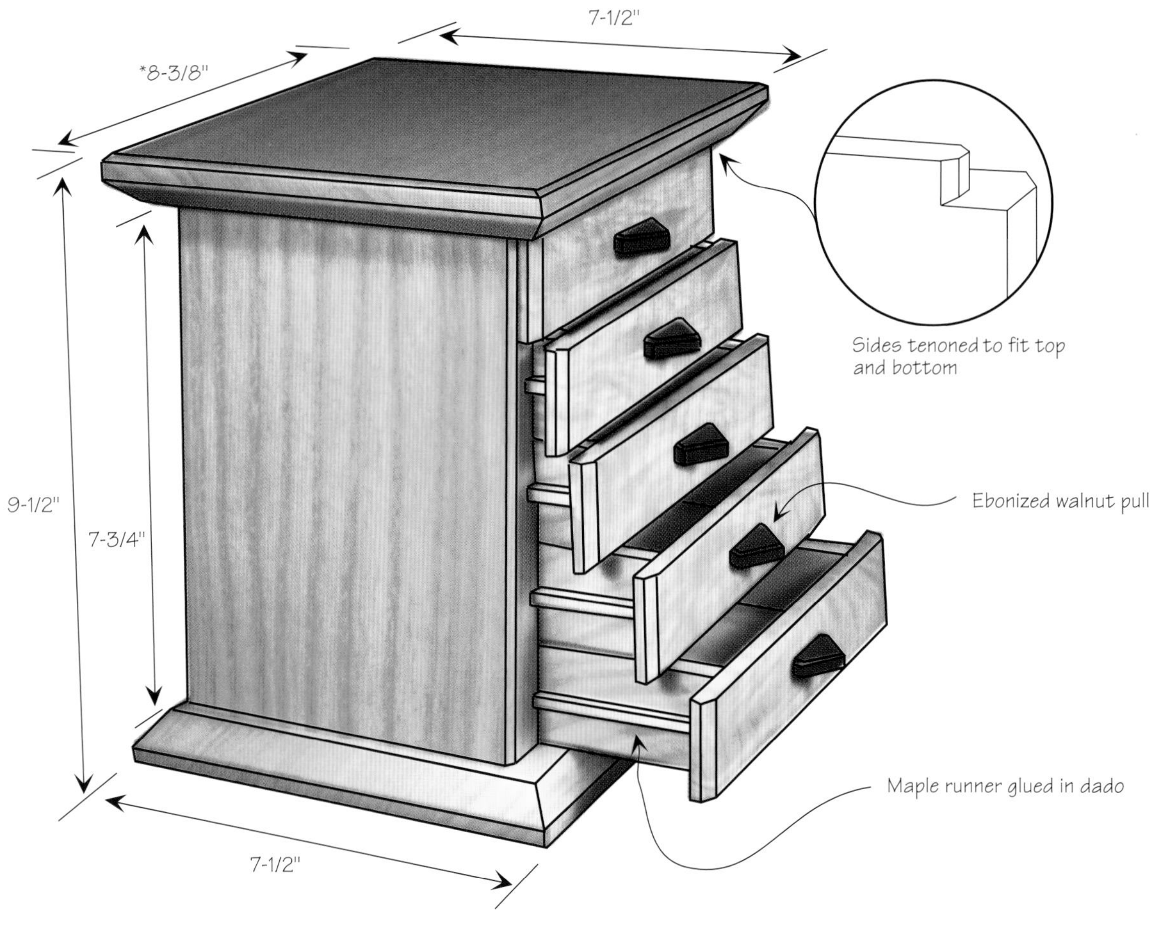

Bill of Materials

PART NAME	NUMBER	DIMENSION TWL	COMMENTS
Top and Bottom	2	7/8 x 7 3/4 x 9	Cut smaller after mortises are cut
Sides	2	1 1/16 x 5 3/4 x 8 1/4	Length includes 1/4" tenons
Back Panel	1	3/8 x 6 x 8 1/8	
Drawer Parts			
Fronts	5	3/8 x 1 1/2 x 7 1/2	
Sides	10	3/8 x 1 1/2 x 5 9/16	Includes 3/16" tenon
Backs	5	3/8 x 1 1/2 x 5 1/4	Includes 3/16" tenons
Drawer Guides	10	3/16 x 5/16 x 5 5/16	
Drawer Pulls	5	5/16 x 1 1/4 x 2	Cut from walnut stock

1 Use a 3/16" straight cut bit to cut the top and bottom mortises. With stops clamped to the fence to control the length of the mortises, lower the workpiece over the moving bit and move it between stops.

2 Using the table saw, begin cutting the tenons on the box sides. The first cut is made with the workpiece flat on the table saw.

3 Adjust the height of cut and position of the table saw fence to finish cutting the tenons. I prefer to cut a test piece first to check for an accurate fit in the mortises.

4 After forming the tenons on the box sides and trimming the tenons to width, draw a line to follow on the band saw, tapering the box sides. The exact angle is not critical to the design, but both sides should match.

Construction Notes

I resawed 2¼" solid stock into halves each 1⅛" thick. You will need 5/4 stock to make this box or adjust the sides and bottom to use narrower stock and change the angle of the sides.

Make the Carcass

Rout the mortises in the top and bottom of the box. Use the router table and 3/16" spiral cutter to rout the mortises to a ¼" depth. Use stop blocks clamped to the fence to control the lengths of the mortises, and check their depth with a dial caliper (see photo 1). As a variation, you could also build this piece using a biscuit joiner #20 biscuits.

Cut the tenons on the box sides. Because of the amount of material that must be removed, it is safest to do this job on the table saw by making cuts as shown in photos 2 and 3. Fit the tenon into the mortise to check the fit (it's helpful to use a test piece to check the fit before cutting the real thing).

With a straight rule, mark the angle on the sides. Then with the band saw, cut the sides to shape (see photo 4).

Rout the sides for the back panel to fit. Use the 3/16" bit in the router table and raise the bit to ¼" height above the table. Then change the fence location, and rout the top and bottom for the back panel to fit.

With a 3/16" bit, rout the drawer guide channels in the box sides. Use stop blocks to prevent routing through the dado for holding the back panel in place. Make the back panel using the

5 Reduce the proportion of the box top by cutting on the sled with the stop block. This must be done after the mortises are cut. Reducing the size of the top keeps the box from feeling top heavy.

6 Use a 45° chamfering bit to rout the front edge of the chest top, but use the table saw at an angle to shape the ends.

7 Use a sanding block to sand the chamfers to keep the edges crisp. By using a series of sanding grits, the hand sanding goes very quickly.

8 In fitting the drawer sides, work from the bottom up, carefully measuring and adjusting the router table fence as needed to cut the channels for the drawer guides to fit. Glue the drawer guides to the drawers after fitting is complete.

same technique used in making the top panel for the Lucy's Jewelry Box. Then cut the top to size, trimming from each end (see photo 5).

With a 45° chamfering bit, rout the profile of the base, and the front and back of the top (the ends need to be cut on the table saw as shown in photo 6). Hand-sanding the base and top will keep the edges crisp (see photo 7).

Assembly

Sand all the parts of the box carcass prior to assembly. Then with a squeeze bottle, apply glue to the inside of the mortises before assembly, but don't glue the back panel in place, as it needs to be left free to expand and contract. With several clamps, hold the chest together as the glue dries. Scrap hardboard between the clamps and the chest itself will prevent marring the surfaces.

Make the Drawers

Each of the drawers is the same width, although they appear to taper along with the shape of the cabinet. To build the drawers, first resaw the material for drawer fronts, backs and sides (I used ash for the interior drawer parts). After cutting the parts to length, rout the mortises in the box sides and front. Follow the same procedure you used in making the box ends for the Inlaid Walnut Ring Box.

Using the router table and fence with a 1" straight cut bit, cut the tenons at the ends of the box back and sides to fit the mortises. Rout the fronts, backs and sides for the box bottoms to fit. Set the ⅛" bit to a ⅛" height, ⅛" from the fence.

Rout the drawer sides with the 3⁄16" straight-cut bit for the drawer guides to fit. Check the fit of the drawers one at a time, and adjust the dado for the drawer guides as needed for proper clearance before the drawers are assembled (see photo 8).

Sand the inside of the drawer front, and the inside and outside of the drawer sides, back and bottom. Assemble them with glue in the mortises, then clamp them together with bar clamps,

9 Starting at the top of the chest, mark the drawers for cutting to width and angle to conform to the sides of the chest.

10 Use simple tacked-in-place strips on the sled to position the drawers at the right angle. The two strips are at opposing angles for cutting the opposite sides of the drawer.

11 Use the sled to cut the drawer pulls to shape after the tenons are formed. The small clamp and stop blocks hold the pull safely, allowing the fingers to be well out of the way of the saw blade.

checking to make certain they are square.

Cut ³⁄₁₆" × ⅜" strips to use as drawer guides. With a ³⁄₁₆" bit, rout the drawer sides for the drawer guides to fit. Routing test pieces will help in aligning the drawers to fit.

Before cutting the drawer fronts to length and angle to match the cabinet sides, rout for the drawer pulls to fit. Then after putting the drawer in place in the cabinet, use a pencil to mark the position of the cabinet side on the back of the drawer front (see photo 9). With the sled on the table saw, use blocking to set up the angle of cut. Align the pencil mark with the far side of the saw kerf so that the drawers will be ⅛" narrower than the total width of the chest (see photo 10).

Finish the Chest

Make your drawer pulls. The triangle shape that I used is designed to go with the angular shape of the jewelry chest (see photo 11). Finally, use Danish oil to finish all the parts and bring out the rich warm color of the natural wood.

Oops!

Being a human being, I make mistakes. Being a successful craftsman implies that I am able to recover from them, possibly learn something from them, and on occasion be inspired by them. I'm not telling you this as an excuse. It is always a blow to my self-esteem when I cut things too short, when I drop something and damage a newly finished piece, or when I glue something together and then find later that it is out of square. It can make a person want to scream and throw things. As a fellow craftsman I hope you will understand that we are all human and that we can fix the things we mess up. Here are a few tips for fixing some of the things that can go wrong.

One of the best ways to avoid making mistakes and ruining important parts is to use scrap to test tool setups before risking your precious hardwoods.

Check wood carefully for cracks and splits that might cause problems in the finished piece. Sometimes, however, they will appear later, or the special character in the wood demands that a particular piece be used despite its flaws. Cracks and splits can be easy to fix. A business card with glue spread on both sides can be slipped into a crack or other hard-to-reach places. You may need to use a small chisel to widen the crack for the card to be inserted. When you pull the card out, the glue remains, and the crack can be clamped closed until the glue has set.

Small chips or gaps can be filled with a mixture of sanding dust from the same wood and clear Duco cement. Mix up a thick paste by adding a squirt of glue to a small pile of sanding dust. Stir it thoroughly into a thick paste. Use a thin piece of hardwood to force it into place. It dries quickly, so it can be sanded flush with the surrounding surface in about 15 minutes, and unlike many fill materials, this one can be finished with Danish oil. Be sure to sand away any glue residue left on the surface.

Shallow dents can be steamed away. Wet the dent and surrounding area with water or spit and then use a hot iron directly on the wood to turn the water to steam. This technique works best where the fibers of wood are not broken, but is worth trying on more severe dents, as well. It can even work on areas that are already finished with Danish oil. On already finished wood, you may want to sand lightly with 320-grit sandpaper after steaming and then apply a fresh coat of Danish oil. But be careful not to leave the iron on the wood too long, as it can scorch.

Occasionally, I've glued up boxes in a hurry and found out later that they were not square. To remedy the problem, put a little water in each corner, and place the box in the microwave for 30 to 45 seconds. The water will turn to steam and soften the glue so the box can be reshaped to square. This will also work if the box needs to be taken apart for repair. The glue will soften enough that the parts can be gently pulled apart and then glued back together with fresh glue. A word of caution: any boxes going in the microwave should not have metal parts like hinges, hinge pins, screws or nails.

Chapter 13

Triangle Tower

Many of my designs start as mere basic sketches, with many of the details unresolved, as I find it easier to assemble elements of a design and then play with the parts to develop the finished concept. This project changed several times as it evolved, and took almost a year of play to reach its finished form. The triangular trays are made of sassafras, with walnut splines, or slip feathers, joining the corners. The trays pivot on a brass welding rod, swinging forward to reveal their contents. It is a challenge to a person's self-confidence to embark on a project not knowing exactly how it will look when completed. Taking risks in design often leads to failure. But without the willingness to risk failure, new things would never be created.

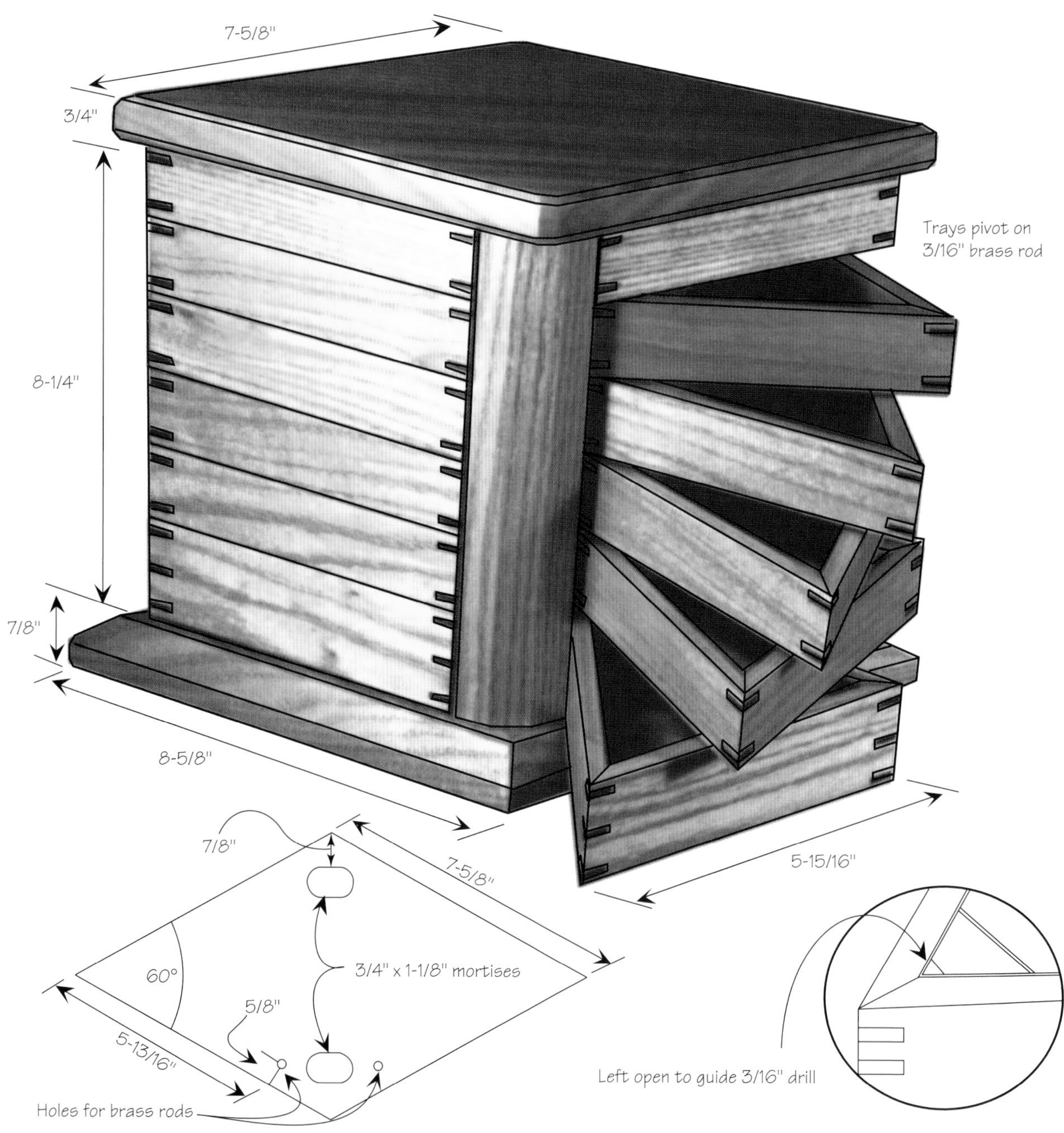

Template for Routing Mortises

Bill of Materials

PART NAME	NUMBER	DIMENSION TWL	COMMENTS
Bottom trays	6	5/16 x 1 3/4 x 5 15/16	
Middle trays	24	5/16 x 1 1/4 x 5 15/16	
Top trays	6	5/16 x 1 1/8 x 5 15/16	
Corner Triangles	12	3/4 long	Make from 11/16 stock
Bottoms	12	5 5/8 on long side	Size is prior to final shaping. Cut from 1/8" x 4"-wide Baltic birch. Final shape requires template routing.
Base	4	1 x 1 7/8 x 8 5/8	Cut angle 30° at one end, 60° at other
Panel	1	1/8 Baltic Birch	Cut from stock 6" x 10 x 1/2"
Top	1	7/8 x 7 1/2 x 13 1/4	Cut as shown in technical art
Vertical stretchers	2	1 x 1 3/4 x 9 1/2	Includes 5/8"-long tenons and each end
Hardware			
Hinge rods	2	3/16 dia. x 9 1/2	Make from brass welding rod
Steel Washers	14	1/4	Paint black
Wood screws	4	#6 x 1 5/8 long	Flat head

1 Clamp the box sides firmly in place as they are cut to length. Use a sled, adjustable fence stop block. A simple cam clamp holds the stock tightly to the fence.

2 Spread glue on the corners . . .

3 . . . and use rubber bands to hold the parts securely as the glue sets.

Make the Triangles

After planing the tray side stock to its finished size, cut the parts to length using the adjustable sled on the table saw. The stop block clamped in position insures uniform length of the parts (see photo 1). Then glue the sides together to make the triangles, using rubber bands to hold the sides together as the glue dries (see photos 2, 3).

Use the slip feather jig on the router table to cut for the walnut splines to fit. Make a sliding tray at the correct angle to hold the corners as they are routed (see photo 4).

4 Use the slip-feather jig on the router table to cut for the slip feathers to fit. The length of the dowel between the workpiece and the fence will position the cut. For subsequent cuts, the dowel can be cut shorter.

5 Use the sled to cut the small slip feathers from solid stock. Turn the walnut stock over between each cut. The push stick keeps the fingers safely away from the blade.

6 With glue spread in the slot and on the slip feathers, "slip" them in place.

7 Use the 6" x 48" belt sander to sand the slip feathers flush with the sides.

8 Cut corner blocks for the triangle drawer units. Use a fence and stop block on the table saw fence, and a push stick.

9 Use V-blocks and C-clamps to glue the corner blocks in place. Carefully align the edges as the parts are assembled.

10 Drill for the pivot rod to fit the triangle trays. Leave a slight space in the corner so that when the corner block is fitted, a natural point of travel is allowed for the drill bit to keep it from wandering.

11 Use a pilot point router bit to cut the ¼"-wide by ⅛"-deep rabbets for the tray bottoms to fit.

Cut triangle wedges to fit the slots, and glue them in place (see photos 5 & 6). Then sand the outside surfaces of the triangle trays so that the wedges are flush (see photo 7).

Glue the corner blocks in place. Note the v-block used to protect the tip of the triangle from clamping pressure (see photos 8, 9). With a drill press, drill the corners for the 3⁄16" brass rod to fit (see photo 10).

Rout the recess for the box bottom to fit, using a rabbeting bit. I used a rabbeting set that included an oversized bearing to allow the very small cut required (see photo 11).

Shape the box bottoms with a template-following router bit. Use a simple frame to hold the bottom panel and template together for routing (see photo 12).

12 Shape a template piece to fit the tray bottom, then use it as a guide for shaping the box bottoms. The V block holds the pieces in alignment with the template without clamping.

Make the Base

The base is constructed of four pieces of 2"-wide sassafras stock and uses the bottom panel as a spline connecting the parts. As in cutting the parts for the triangle trays, use the adjustable angle sled to cut the parts to size (you'll need to change the angle to cut the opposite ends to length).

Use a ⅛"-kerf saw blade and with the blade height raised to about 1½", stand the bottom parts on edge along the fence and cut for the bottom panel to fit. Use the sled to cut the bottom panels to size.

Rout and sand the inside edges of the sassafras parts and the bottom panel prior to gluing. Then squeeze glue into the saw kerf and assemble the parts around the bottom panel. Use a band clamp to hold the parts in alignment as the glue sets (see photo 13).

Make the Tower Top

Cut and plane sassafras stock to oversize dimension, and then using the angle sled on the table saw, trim the top piece to size. At the same time, cut a template piece to size from scrap plywood. This will be used for routing the mortises into the top and bottom of the cabinet.

With a plunge router and a ⅝" straight-cut bit, rout the locations for the mortises in the plywood template according to the measurements given in the drawing. Clamp the template to the top of the underside of the tower and, using the ½" mortise cleanup bit in the plunge router, rout the mortises for the vertical stretchers to fit to a depth of about ⅝".

Position the template on the base and rout the mortises in it. Turn the template over between routing the top and the bottom to make sure the bottom is the mirror image of the top (see photo 14). To accommodate the brass rods, drill the 3⁄16" holes into the top. Drill the same holes in the template and then use the template to mark and drill the holes in the bottom (see photo 15).

13 To make the base for the triangle tower, cut parts to shape and use a chamfering bit to shape the inside edges. The ⅛" birch plywood bottom also serves as a spline holding the sides together. Spread glue on the ends and use a band clamp to hold the parts together while the glue dries.

14 Use a template-following mortise cleanup bit to cut the mortises in the bottom and top of the triangle tower. Clamp the template in place and then, using a plunge router, gradually lower the cutter into the work piece.

15 With pivot pin holes drilled in the template, and with the vertical stretchers in place, mark the locations for the pivot holes in the base and top of the triangle tower.

Make the Vertical Stretchers

Measure the heights of the trays including the washers used as spacers between them. Also measure the heights of the top and bottom. Cut the vertical stretchers to that length plus 1¼" for the two ⅝" tenons to fit the top and bottom.

Cut tenons on the ends of the vertical stretchers using the table saw and the sled or the tenoning jig. Use a rasp to then round the corners of the tenons. To ease the process, you can also use a band saw to cut 45° shoulders from the tenons (see photo 16).

The vertical stretcher at the front will have to be routed to provide clearance for the trays to pivot when opened. Use a core-box bit in the router table to form the curved portion of the clearance. Then use the table saw to finish the cut. Rout the remaining edges with a chamfering bit.

Assemble the Triangle Tower

Cut the brass rod to length, then bevel the ends on the belt and disc sander. Rout the edges of the top, bottom and vertical stretchers with a chamfering bit. Sand all the parts starting with 150-grit and finishing with 320. Glue the tray bottoms in place, and then use Danish oil to finish all the parts.

Align the trays along the brass rods using the brass washers between trays (see photo 17). After spreading glue in the mortises, assemble the triangle towers and clamp them together until the glue dries.

With a template the same size and shape as the inside of the trays, use a rotary cutter to cut the lining material to size and, with white glue, glue them in place.

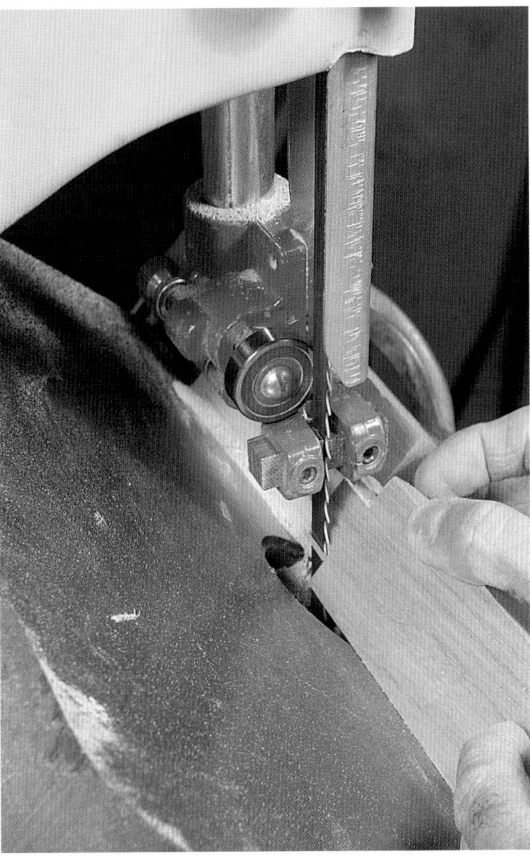

16 **After cutting the tenons on the table saw, use the band saw with its table at a 45° angle to trim the corners of the tenons prior to rasping.**

17 **As the triangle tower is assembled, use paste wax to lubricate the pivot rod. Place washers between the parts to provide clearance for opening.**

Chapter 14

Tribute to American Linden

I believe the job of an artist is to use his or her tools of expression to help others connect with the world. We often discover value in things only after they have been pointed out to us as having value. This box is intended as my tribute to American linden, commonly known as basswood. While technically a hardwood, it is softer than many softwoods, and takes carving details easily. My wood carving skills are somewhat limited. But woodcarving does not need to be highly refined in order to be effective. Using simple techniques we can express things of importance in our lives, illustrating our connections with each other, and with the natural world.

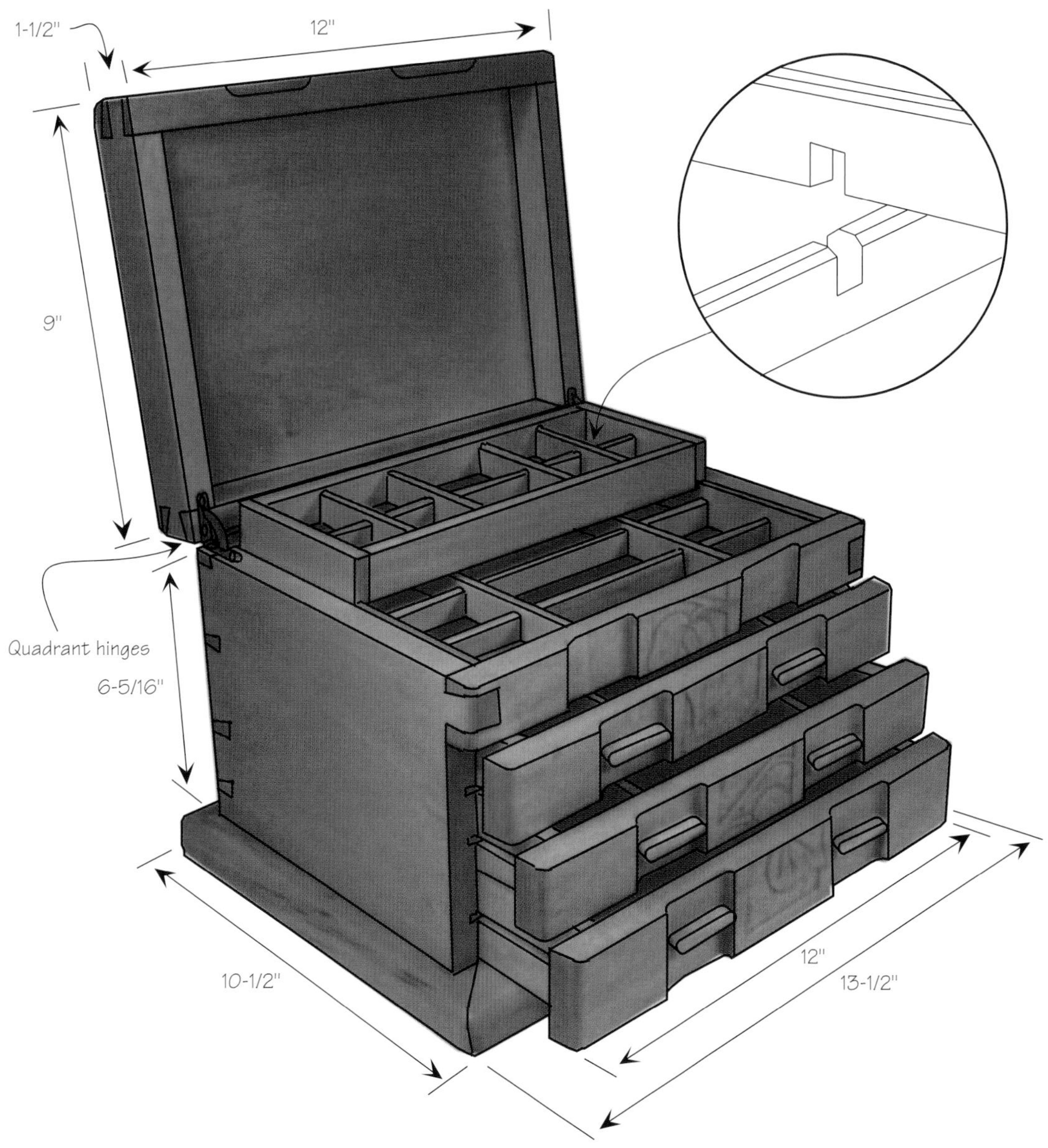
1-1/2"
12"
9"
Quadrant hinges
6-5/16"
10-1/2"
12"
13-1/2"

1 Use a simple template and bowl cutting router bit to form the shape of the front of the chest.

Making the Box

This project is made with hand-cut dovetails and carved with a simple relief pattern of leaves, twigs and fruit modeled after the simple line drawings in one of my favorite books, *Trees of Arkansas* by Dwight Moore. In selecting the parts for this box, I wanted the front to be from a single board and matched to the sides and back. I therefore used stock wide enough to allow for the saw kerfs when cutting and separating the drawers.

Shape the Front of the Box

Make a template for routing the recess that will not only house the pulls, but also define the areas for carving and provide the lift area for the lid. Use scrap material to "build" the form by overlapping and nailing corners.

Clamp the template in place and, using a bowl-cutting bit with a guide bearing, rout the recess at one side. Change the location of the template, and rout the other side (see photo 1). Sand the interior spaces of the shaped areas. Then cut the drawer fronts from the box-front stock, leaving the box front remaining.

Joint the Corners

When cutting the dovetails, some craftsmen prefer to cut the pins first and then the tails; others like me, do the opposite. Mark out the location of the tails using a sliding T-bevel, a small square, a pencil, and a marking gauge (see photo 2, 3).

Bill of Materials

PART NAME	NUMBER	DIMENSION TWL	COMMENTS
Sides	2	3/4 x 8 x 9 1/16	
Front	1	3/4 x 8 1/4 x 12 1/16	before cutting of drawer fronts
Top panel	1	1/2 x 8 1/16 x 11 1/16	
Bottom	1	1/4 x 8 1/16 x 1 1/16	Baltic birch plywood
Dividers	3	1/4 x 3/4 x 10 1/4	
Dividers	2	1/4 x 7/8 x 7 9/16	
Base	2	7/8 x 1 5/8 x 13 1/2	
Base	2	7/8 x 1 5/8 x 10 1/2	
Bottom	1	1/8 x 9 1/8 x 12 1/8	Baltic birch plywood
Upper Drawers			
Facings	2	3/4 x 1 1/2 x 12	
Sides	4	7/16 x 1 1/2 x 7 13/16	Includes 1/4" tenon
Backs	2	7/16 x 1 1/2 x 10 1/16	Includes 1/4" tenons
Bottoms	2	1/4 x 7 1/2 x 10	Baltic birch plywood
Dividers	4	1/4 x 7/8" x 9 9/16	
Dividers	4	1/4 x 1 1/8" x 7 1/8	
Lower Drawer			
Facing	1	3/4 x 1 15/16 x 12	
Sides	2	7/16 x 1 15/16 x 7 13/16	Includes 1/4" tenon
Back	1	7/16 x 1 15/16 x 10 1/16	Includes 1/4" tenons
Bottom	1	1/4 x 7 1/2 x 10	Baltic birch plywood
Trays			
Sides	2	5/16 x 1 1/8 x 4 1/16	
Front	1	5/16 x 1 1/8 x 10 1/16	Includes 1/8" tenons
Back	1	5/16 x 1 1/8 x 10 1/16	Includes 1/8" tenons
Slides	2	3/16 x 1 x 7 9/16	
Dividers	1	1/4 x 5/8 x 9 13/16	
Dividers	4	1/4 x 13/16 x 3 11/32	
Hardware			
Pulls	6	3/16" x 1/2" x 1 3/4"	
Quadrant Hinges	1 pr.		
Flathead Screws	6	#6 x 1 5/8"	

2 & 3 Use a sliding T bevel, a marking gauge and square to lay out the dovetails. Note that the drawer front parts have been ripped from the other portion of the front of the chest.

4 Use a sharp chisel to remove the waste between the dovetails.

5 Use a chisel to clean up the sides of the tails. I do this to square the edges and remove the saw marks.

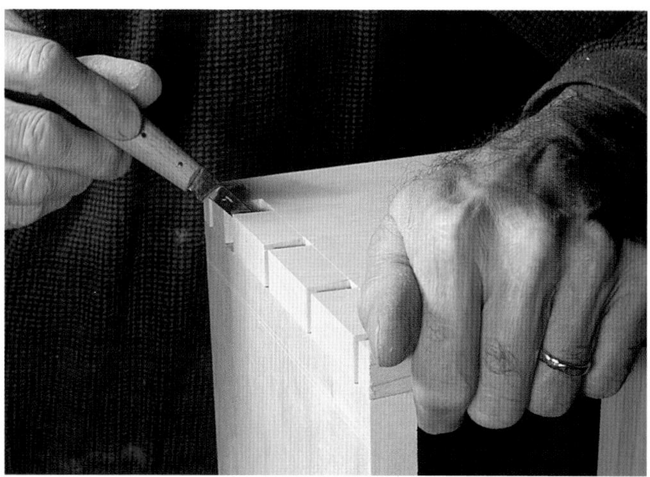

6 Use a sharp knife to mark the shape of the pins directly from the cut tails.

7 Use a chisel to remove the waste between the pins. Make your final shearing cut by using the marking gauge scored line to position the chisel.

For cutting the tails, my preference is to use a Japanese Dozuki saw, whose teeth cut on the pull rather than the push. When laying out the tails, be careful to allow for the saw kerf, which will be cut away when separating the lid from the body of the box.

Chisel the waste from between the tails. American linden is very soft and easy to chisel (see photo 4). To keep the edges crisp and clean, make your first cuts away from the marking gauge lines, and then when most of the stock has been removed, align the chisel with the marked lines to make the final cuts (see photo 5).

Use the cut tails to mark where the pins will be cut. I use a small chip-carving knife rather than a pencil because the cut line conforms more closely to the shape of the tails (see photo 6). Place the tailed stock in position over the end of the pin stock, and trace the shape of the tails with the knife. Use the Dozuki saw to cut the shape of the pins, and chisel away the remaining waste. Cut only the inside portion of the top tails, leaving some to be cut away for the mitered corners. I don't spend enough time cutting dovetails to be perfect at it, and I always seem to spend some time monkeying with the final fit (see photo 7).

Use the 45° sled on the table saw to cut the miters in the top corners and, with the table saw, cut the box sides to allow for the drawers to fit. But be careful not to cut all the way through. Finish the cut with the dozuki saw and chisel it smooth by holding the chisel flat against the sawn surface.

With the router table fence and a ¼" straight-cut bit, rout the box sides for the drawer guides to fit (see photo 8). Use the Dozuki saw to finish fit the miters at the box corners (see photos 9 & 10).

8 Use the router table and straight-cut router bit to cut the dadoes for the drawer guides, top panel and chest bottom to fit. Adjust the fence to position the cuts and use stop blocks clamped to the table to control the length of the cuts so as not to appear on the outside of the chest.

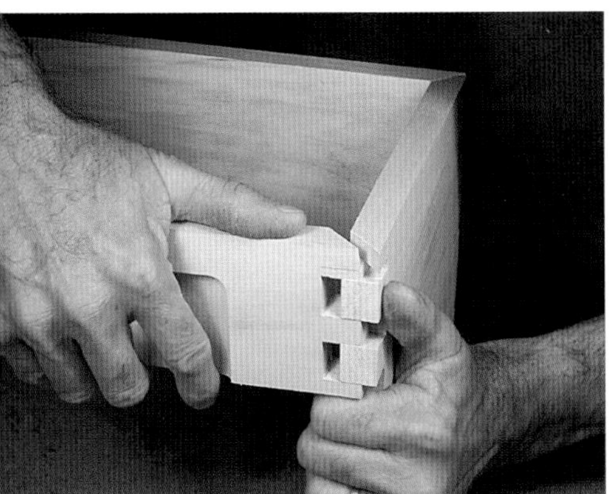

9 After cutting the mitered corners, check the fit of the pins and tails.

10 With the corners pulled almost closed, use the Dozuki saw to clean up the mitered cut. The dovetail joint should be open about a saw kerf wide to bring a perfect fit.

11 Use cutout shapes to design the carved pattern. The heart shape of the American linden leaves makes them appealing for a jewelry box without being trite.

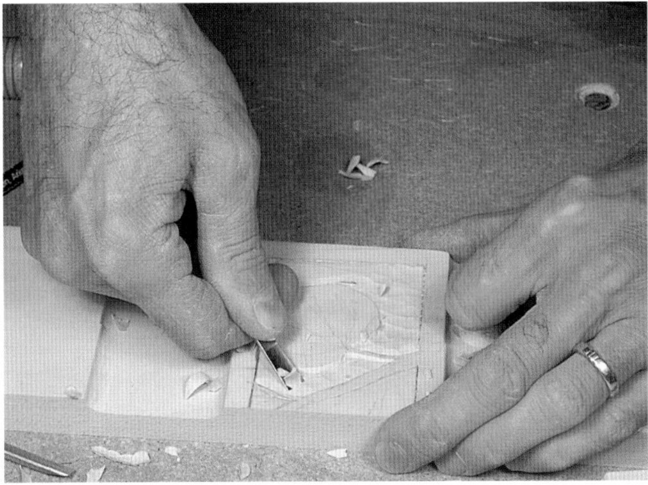

12 Do the carving on the front of the box using a small straight chisel and shallow gouge. I follow the pencil outlines with the straight chisel and then remove the waste between with the gouge.

Make and Fit the Top Panel and Box Bottom

Measure the inside space into which the top will fit, then add ½" to each dimension, reduce the length by 1/32" and the width by 1/16" to allow for clearance, expansion and contraction. Cut the top panel and box bottom to these dimensions.

Rout channels for the top and bottom to fit. Use stops positioned along the router table fence to keep the cut from exiting the workpieces. Then with the table saw, define the tongues on the top panel.

Assembly

Before assembling the box, sand all inside surfaces. Spread glue on the surfaces of the tails and pins where they will meet. Carefully pull the parts into position and clamp if necessary. Check to make sure the box carcass is square. When the glue has dried, sand the dovetails and pins flush with the surrounding wood, and use a ½"-radius roundover bit to give the top corners of the box its finished shape.

Carve the Design

When laying out the design, remember to allow for the saw kerf when the box top is removed from the body. I started my carving on the box before it was assembled to keep from hammering too much on the assembled box. Position the various drawer fronts and the box front in order so the sketch of the carving will cover all the parts. I use cut out shapes of leaves to achieve a pattern (see photos 11, 12, 13). The leaves can be folded and traced to form different shapes and changed in size and orientation to create a pleasing design. Use a pencil to sketch in the branches (pencil lines can be erased easily from the basswood, so play with the design until you find one that you like). Remember that skill in design is like every other

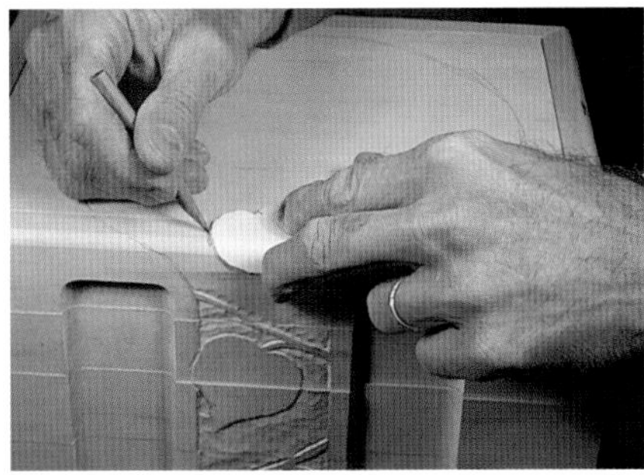

13 The paper template bends easily to carry the design up and over the front edge of the box and onto the top.

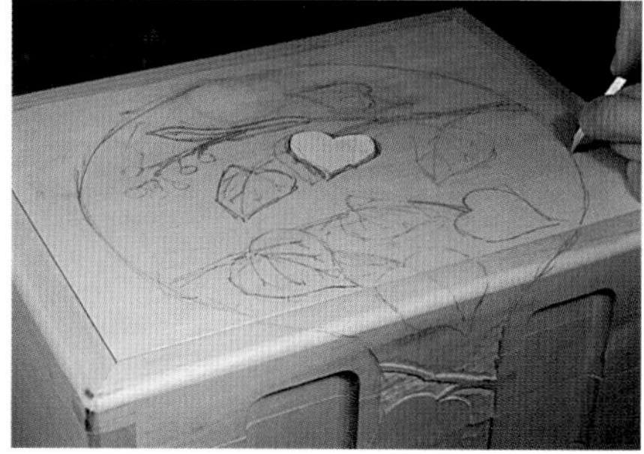

14 & 15 Use the straight chisel to outline the design elements and then the gouge to define the space between.

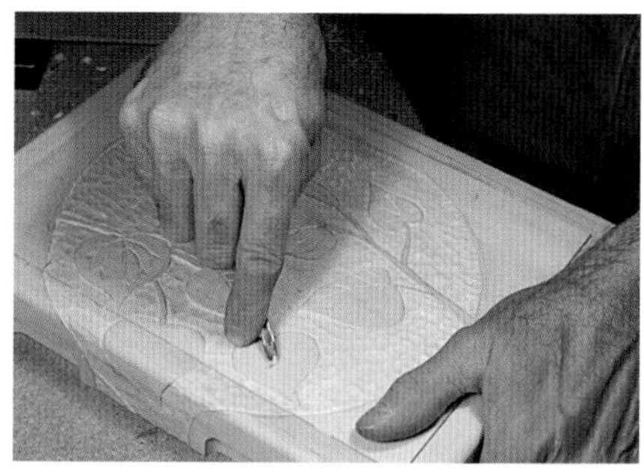

16 Use other chisels to give detail to the carving. Here I use a V-groove gouge to add veins in a leaf.

17 Hand sanding completes the carving by gently rounding sharp edges and smoothing the background.

18 A relief cut made on the table saw eases the cut in forming the tenons. The safety blocking has been removed to show the process more clearly.

thing you will learn in woodworking. It will evolve with time and experience. You may find it easier to develop a design for carving from a line drawing than from a photograph, so a trip to the library may be useful. Use a small straight chisel to cut the outline of the carving (see photos 14, 15). Most of my carving is done with a straight chisel and a very shallow gouge that I use to carve away the background areas (see photo 16).

Continue the design on the lid of the box, beginning at the box front, rounding up over the front edge and into the top panel. Use the same leaf shapes and sketched branches. I added the linden berries to conform to the line drawing shown in *Trees of Arkansas*, and to add interest to the design. Sand the background with a range of grits moving from coarse to fine. The sanding will soften some of the crisp edges. I use handheld sandpaper rather than a power sander which would quickly remove essential details (see photo 17).

Make the Drawers

Use the same mortise-and-tenon technique as was used in making the Inlaid Walnut Ring box to fit the drawer sides to the drawer fronts and backs. With a 3/16" straight-cut bit, rout the mortises into the drawer fronts, then adjust the fence position and rout the mortises in the box sides.

Use a 1" straight cut router bit to form the tenons on the drawer sides and backs (see photo 18). Use a 1/8" straight-cut bit to rout for the drawer bottoms to fit. Then with a 3/16" straight-cut bit in the router table, rout the drawer sides to fit the hardwood drawer guides in the box (see photo 19).

Before routing the drawer sides, place the drawer guides in position in the box sides. Carefully measure and cut test pieces to check the fit of the drawer sides before actually routing the channels.

19 Check the fit of the drawer guides before the drawers are assembled. I rout test pieces and check the fit before routing the guide channels in the drawer sides.

Cut the drawer bottoms to size, then sand all the inside surfaces of the drawer parts. Assemble the drawers, using glue spread in the mortises (make sure you check for square).

20 Shape the front edge of the base to reflect the front of the chest by using the router table and straight-cut bit. Remove the waste first with the band saw.

21 Assemble the parts of the base around the birch plywood panel. The birch plywood serves as both the bottom of the chest and as the spline holding the parts of the base together.

22 Make the template for installing the hinges by using the router table and fence with stop blocks to control the cut. Make two identical pieces. One will be used to make the guide for the left hinge and the other for the right. Additional templates will be needed to rout clearance for the integral lid stops.

23 Rout for the left and right hinges to fit. I always do a test piece first to make sure the depth is correct. I use a ¼" router bit and 7/16" guide bushing in a ½" wide template to cut the space required for a 5/16" wide hinge.

Then rout the drawer fronts for the drawer pulls to fit.

Use the router table to rout the front of the base to reflect the shape of the box front. I used a ¾"-radius straight-cut router bit in the router table along with the fence and stop blocks to position the cut (see photo 20). The parts of the base are assembled using the same technique used in making the base for the Triangle Tower (see photo 21).

I chose to use very simple pulls modeled after the dividers used in the Men's Jewelry box. They are simple pieces of maple, with the ends rounded on the router table and the top edges slightly rounded with sandpaper.

Use the techniques shown in earlier chapters to make the sliding tray and dividers for the top and drawers. Use quadrant hinges to attach the lid. There are ready-made jigs to assist in installing these hinges, but I chose to make my own. I started with a piece of ¼" Baltic birch plywood and used a ½" straight-cut bit in the router table with stop blocks to control the position of the cut (see photo 22). Since quadrant hinges require matching left- and right-hand sides, you'll need separate matching jigs to rout for the support arms to fit.

After nailing parts to the jig to allow it to be clamped in place, use the jig to rout in the box corners for the hinges to fit (see photos 23 & 24). This technique requires a ¼" straight-cut router bit and a 7/16" guide bushing. Finally, use screws to attach the base to the carcass after the box is finished and oiled.

24 Next, rout the clearance required for the stop arms with the plunge router and ⅛" bit. Each side should be routed to just over half the length of the stop arm.

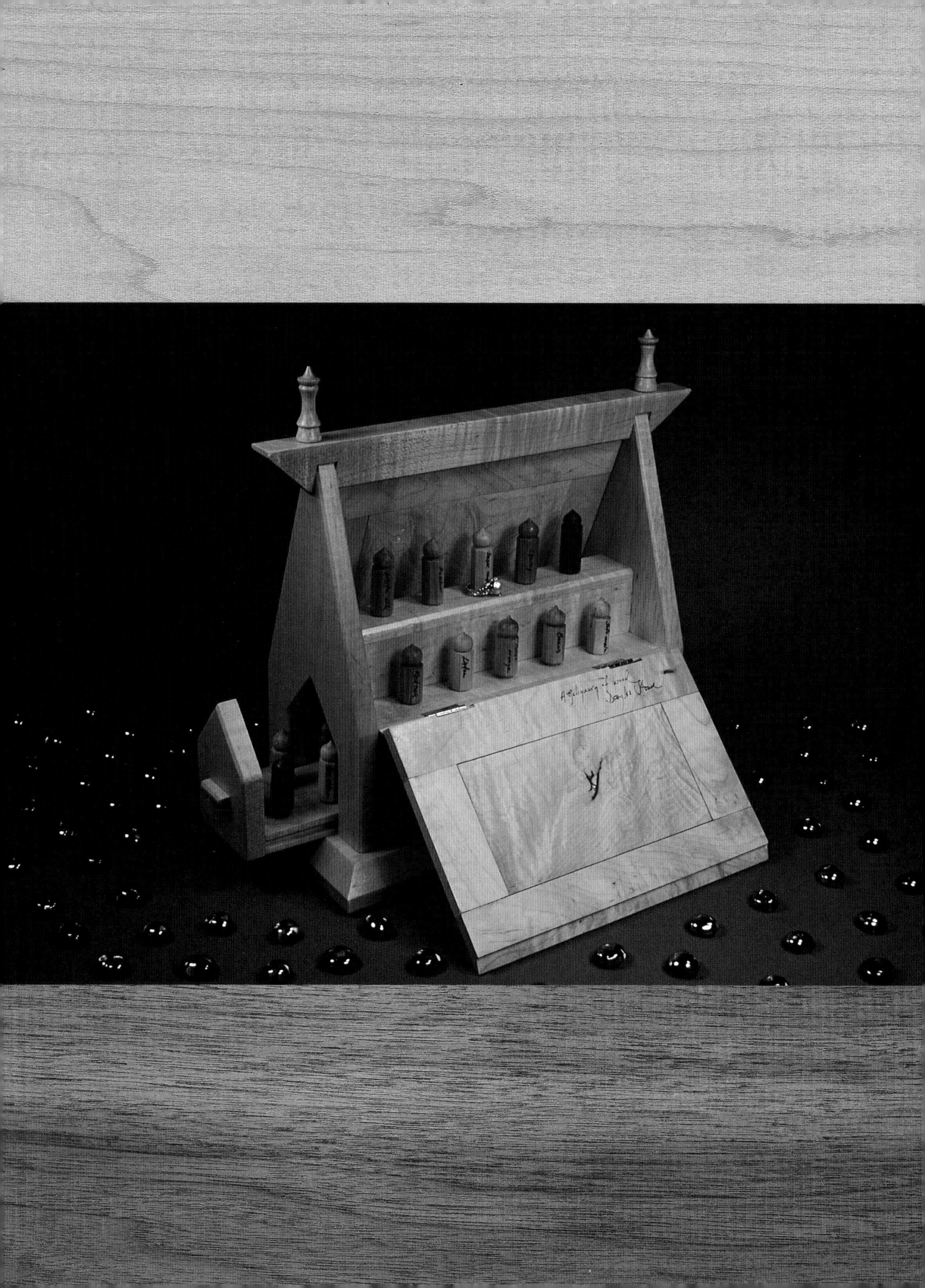

Chapter 15

A Reliquary of Wood

I like to look for inspiration outside the woodworking realm. One of my favorite places in the world is the Nelson-Atkins Museum in Kansas City, as it has a great collection of Chinese furniture. My wife and daughter went there with me to celebrate my fiftieth birthday. At the time, I was working on this book and had also been invited to make a "shrine" for inclusion in an exhibit with other craft artists. In a museum case I discovered a small tin box, beautifully painted, simple, elegant and made to hold precious religious relics. That reliquary is the inspiration for this box, which is made to hold turned and labeled samples of Arkansas hardwoods. It can also be used to hold and display rings.

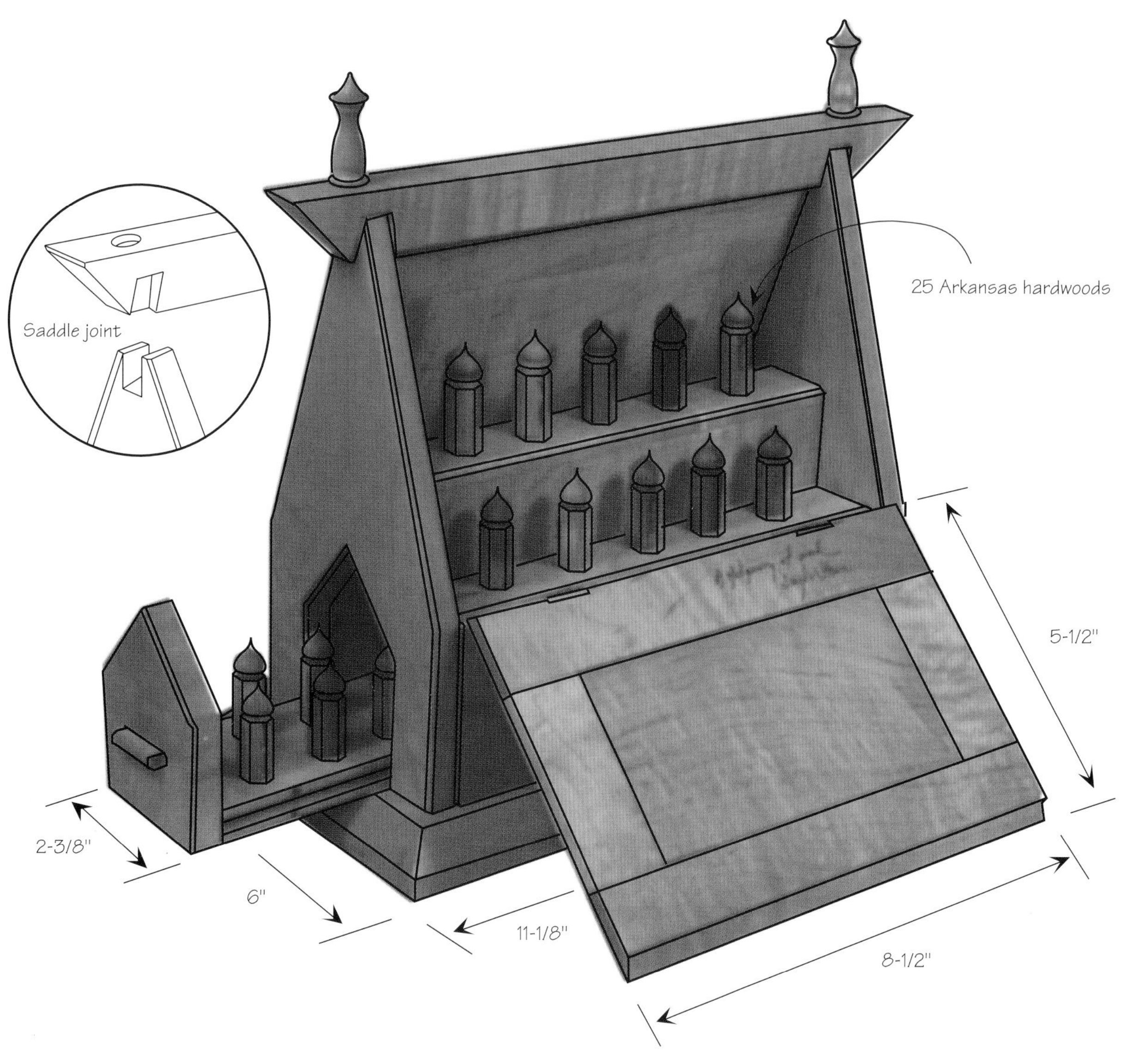
Saddle joint
25 Arkansas hardwoods
5-1/2"
2-3/8"
6"
11-1/8"
8-1/2"

Making the Reliquary

The reliquary is made of sugar maple and uses a mortise-and-tenon technique as used in making the Inlaid Walnut Ring Box. It's made to hold fifteen wood samples or rings in the upper section and an additional ten in the drawers that open at each end. To prevent warping, the lids they are made with floating panels in a frame held together with mortise-and-tenon joints.

This is a more complicated box, but it uses many of the techniques covered in earlier projects. Rather than cover the making of the entire box, this is an overview of some of the more unusual elements of the process.

I resawed the lumber for the end pieces from 5/4 sugar maple. It is important to note that where parts of differing thicknesses are required, resawing need not be at the center of the stock. Resaw the material on the band saw and, using the thickness planer, bring the stock to the desired thicknesses. I made my box ends from 1/2" stock, the box sides and doors from 3/8" stock and the interior parts from 5/16" and 3/16" stock.

Make the Ends

To save material, cut the parts out so that the point of one box end enters the drawer space of the next (see photos 1, 2). Make preliminary cuts on the band saw to isolate the ends from each other. Then use the sled on the table saw to trim the ends to final size (see photo 3). At the same time, cut a template piece that can be used for routing the inside of the drawer opening and to check the positions of the mortises as they are made. Define the interior shape of the template piece by making cuts with the table saw and the band saw, and finally shaping with a straight chisel and rasp.

Bill of Materials

PART NAME	NUMBER	DIMENSION TWL	COMMENTS
Ends	2	1/2 x 4 1/2 x 8 3/8	
Sides	2	3/8 x 2 7/8 x 9	Includes 1/4" tenons
Interior Parts	1	5/16 x 1 3/8 x 8 3/4	
Interior Parts	2	5/16 x 1 1/4 x 8 3/4	
Interior Parts	2	1/4 x 1 3/8 x 8 1/2	
Drawer Guides	2	1/2 x 1 1/4 x 8 1/2	
Ridge	1	13/16 x 1 1/16 x 12	
Doors	2		
Horizontal Rails	4	3/8 x 1 1/4 x 8 7/16	
Stiles	4	3/8 x 1 1/4 x 4	Includes 1/2" tenons
Panels	2	3/8 x 3 5/32 x 6 7/32	Includes 1/8" tongues on panel edges
Drawer			
Facings	2	1/2 x 2 3/8 x 3 5/16	
Bottom	2	1/2 x 2 3/8 x 4 1/2	Includes 1/4" tenon to fit drawer front
Base	1	7/8 x 6 x 11 1/8	
Hardware			
Brass Hinges	2 pr.	1 x 7/8 (open width)	
Exterior Turnings	2		
Hardwood Samples	25		Turned from octagonal stock

1 To make efficient use of materials use the table saw and band saw to make cuts separating the box ends. The point of one end protrudes into the drawer opening of the matching end.

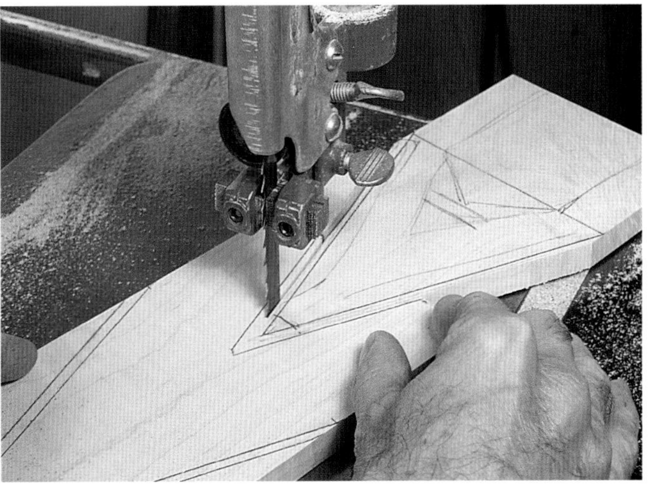

2 Separate the box ends with the band saw.

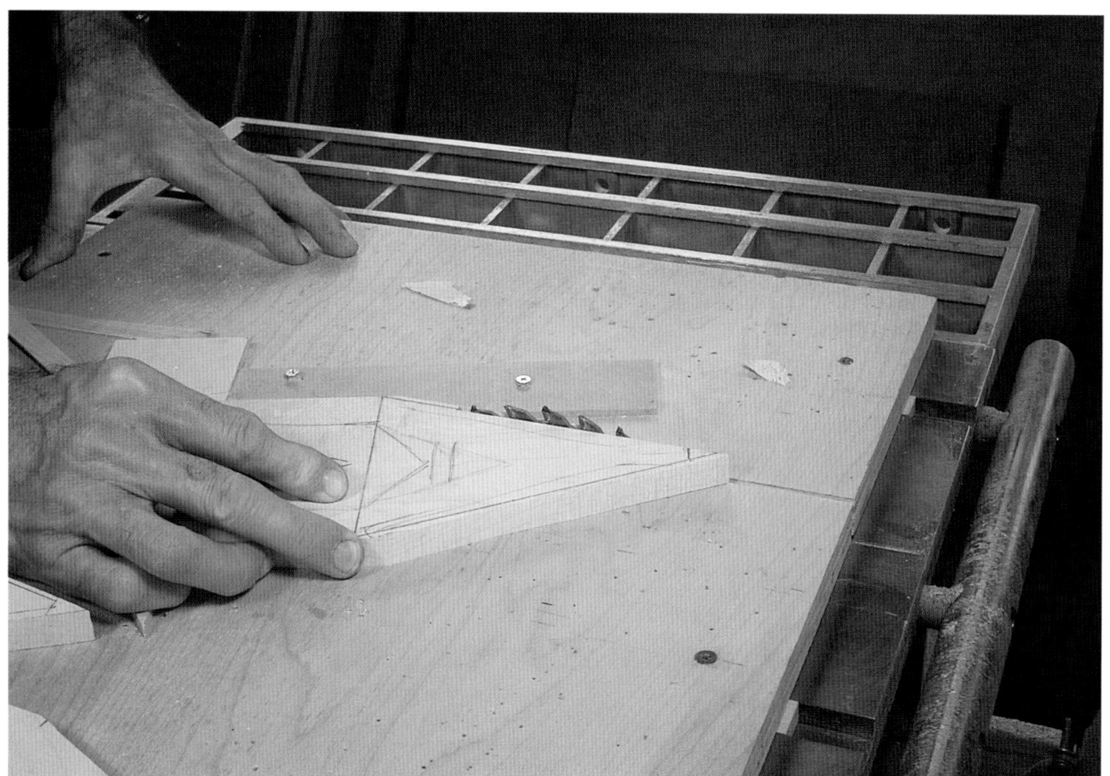

3 Use the sled on the table saw with stop blocks tacked in place to cut the angled rooflines.

4 Use a template-following router bit to shape the interior space of the drawers. Band-saw the rough shape before routing.

5 Use the router table, fence, stop blocks and a ⅛" straight-cut bit to form the mortises for the sides and interior parts to fit.

Use the template-following bit to rout the doorway shapes in the end pieces. First, cut away waste with the band saw to ease the router's work and to prevent tear-out (see photo 4). Use a straight chisel to finish the point of the doorway where the template bit was unable to cut. Then rout the mortises in the end pieces for the sides, internal shelves and drawer guides to fit with a ⅛" router bit, fence and stop blocks on the router table to control the position and length of cut. Rout the mortises to a depth of ¼" for the sides to fit. The mortises for the internal parts should be ⅛" deep (see photo 5).

Cut the saddle joints into the top of the ends. This joint is for the top cross beam to fit. Use the band saw and fence to cut into the top, turning it

6 Use the band saw to form the saddle joint for the top beam to fit. A stop block clamped to the table controls the depth of cut, while the fence controls the width of the opening.

7 Use a chisel to finish the cut.

over to make the opposite cut (see photo 6). I clamped a stop block on the band saw table to control the depth of the cut. Then using a straight chisel, remove the stock between the cuts to finish the joint (see photo 7).

Cut the matching saddle joints in the top beam and then cut it to shape using the table saw and router. To cut the saddle joint, begin with the router table and use a chisel to finish the joint (see photo 8).

8 Use a chisel to finish cutting the saddle joint in the top beam.

9 Use the mortise-and-tenon techniques on the router table and table saw to form the door frames. Then after chamfering the inside edges of the frames, finish the chamfer into the corners with a chisel.

Make the Doors

Mortise and tenon the parts for the doors. Use the router table to rout the mortises following the same steps as used in making the internal parts for the Pin Cabinet, or for the lid for the Cherry Jewelry Chest.

Tenon the side stretchers for the doors using the sled on the table saw or a tenoning jig. Assemble the door parts and, using the chamfering router bit, rout the inside space within the door frame. Then use a sharp chisel to finish the corners. Take the door frames apart and rout the dadoes for the panels to fit (see photo 9).

Make the door panels following the same technique used for making the Wedding Ring Music Box. Use a pilotless V-groove bit to chamfer the edges of the panels. Sand the interior edges and routed chamfers on the door parts and panels and, after putting glue in the mortises, assemble the doors. Clamp the parts while the glue dries.

Make the Sides and Interior Parts

Tenon the sides and internal parts following the same steps as used in some of the earlier boxes. Cut the angles on the interior parts and box sides. Cut matching angles on the assembled doors to fit the sides and top beam.

Cut dadoes on the top shelf for the interior panels to fit. Then cut a tongue on the interior panels sized to fit the dadoes and cut them to fit between the interior shelves.

10 Make a template from scrap stock and use it with a template-following router bit to shape the drawer ends.

Making the Drawers

Cut some maple stock to the required shape (see photo 10). It should be undersized to allow movement in opening and closing. Rout the mortise in the drawer front for the drawer bottom to fit. Tenon the end of the drawer bottom to fit the mortise. Finally, cut drawer guide slots in the drawer sides.

11 Squeeze glue into the mortises in the ends as the reliquary is assembled. It is amazing how many complicated parts are required for a simple design. Careful fitting of parts allows it to go together easily.

Prepare for Assembly

Mark the locations on the interior shelves and drawer bottoms for the wood sample pins to fit. Using a ⅜" bit in the drill press, drill holes about ¼" deep.

Rout the sides and doors for the hinges to fit. Use the router table and a 1" straight-cut bit to cut the hinge mortises. The height of cut should be just under half of the closed thickness of the hinge.

Rout each of the box parts with a slight chamfer, and sand them through a range of grits from coarse to extra fine. Then do the final shaping of the ridge beam and drill it for the turned finials to fit.

Turn the Finials and Posts

Use the four jaw pin chuck on the lathe to turn the finials and interior posts from ½" square stock. Leave most of the posts flat to allow the names of the woods to be inscribed. I use a ⅜" open-end wrench to check the accuracy of the turned tenons for fitting into the holes in the interior shelves. Turn the finials for the top from sugar maple. I chose sugar maple for the finials to leave the brightly colored assortment of woods on the inside a surprise when the reliquary is opened.

Assemble the reliquary (see photo 11) and use Danish oil finish to bring out the natural colors of the woods.

Conclusion

I've met many other woodworkers who when examining my boxes have said, "I just don't have the patience for that sort of work."

Making boxes is a process. It begins with one. Select from the boxes offered in this book to begin your box making adventure, or use the techniques shown here to make boxes of your own design. Feel free to experiment.

It is funny how we will wait "patiently" at a red light, secure in the knowlege it will turn green. Making boxes is the same thing, except that it is best not to wait. Begin! Proceed! Join the ranks of "we that have tried, failed and learned." At some point you will look back to find your own story told in wood.

Index